MRS. BEETON

150 Years of Cookery & Household Management

Graham Nown

WARD LOCK LIMITED · LONDON

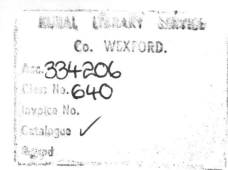
First published in Great Britain in 1986
by Ward Lock Limited, 8 Clifford Street,
London W1, an Egmont Company.

British Library Cataloguing in Publication Data

Nown, Graham
  Mrs Beeton's 150th anniversary.
  1. Beeton, *Mrs*–Influence
  2. Home economics–Great Britain
  –History
  I. Title
  640   TX140.B4

  ISBN 0–7063–6459–7

Printed and bound by Butler & Tanner Ltd., Frome, Somerset.

FOR SYLVANA

Acknowledgments

The author is grateful to Rodney Levick for permission to use Beeton family documents and photographs; Lucy Lunt, BBC Wales, Kitty O'Connor, Killarney Library; Robert Thomson, Harrow Library; Pat Clarke, Pinner Local History Society; Eileen Golborn of Rosemary Books; Wm Collins, Sons & Co Ltd, for permission to quote from Nancy Spain's *Mrs Beeton and Her Husband*; Michael Smith; Denise Carter for sleuthing the pictures; Sylvana Nown for her meticulous historical research and support.

Anyone wishing to delve more deeply into the extraordinary life of Mrs Beeton should read her three excellent biographies – H. Montgomery Hyde's *Mr and Mrs Beeton*; Nancy Spain's *Mrs Beeton and Her Husband*; and Sarah Freeman's definitive *Isabella and Sam*.

The author and publishers are grateful to the following for permission to reproduce photographs in which they hold the copyright:
BBC Hulton Picture Library, page 3, 6, 30, 31, 34, 106; Guildhall Library, page 10; Mansell Collection, page 28, 29, 39, 48, 58, 111; Mary Evans Picture Library, page 36, 45, 46, 72, 103, 109, 112, 113 and 114; National Trust Photographic Library, page 50; Science Museum, page 11, 20; Suffolk Records Office, page 19.

Colour Plate sections: Bridgeman Art Library, Angelo Hornak Picture Library, Longleat House, Mansell Collection, National Trust Photographic Library, the Tate Gallery.

Contents

1
The Real Mrs Beeton

One hundred and fifty years ago, as thirty-five workers signed on at a new factory in Northampton to manufacture the first gas cookers, Isabella Mary Mayson entered the world. The gas cookers and Isabella were both to revolutionize the British kitchen, but nothing before or since has quite eclipsed the influence of the girl who was to become Mrs Beeton.

The name still conjures the image of a humourless matron in a mob-cap, bustling in black bombazine among the mixing bowls and cast-iron pans of a cavernous Victorian kitchen. Many generations after her death few of the thousands of the women who poured avidly over Mrs Beeton's kitchen bible knew who she was, or even if she had existed at all.

In 1922 a worried reader who could find no trace of her in the *Dictionary of National Biography*, the literary hall of fame, wrote to a magazine called *Notes & Queries*: 'Was Beeton the real name of the author of the half-dozen books attributed to the same writer? Is she still alive to enjoy the success of her work? Has she any printed record?'

Ten years later the *Manchester Guardian* attempted to put the record straight: 'Of Mrs Beeton herself more is known, as is only right and proper,' it breezed. 'She was Elizabeth Acton, who was born at Battle, in Sussex, on the 17th day of April, 1799. She passed her early life in Ipswich, and it was in that town that her first volume of verse was published in 1826 . . . '

The *Manchester Guardian* rattled on confidently in this vein for a good half column, unaware that every single fact in the intriguing piece was hopelessly wrong. An apology followed and it took *The Times* to set the record straight. Curious, because the husband and wife team no one could quite place set so many of the standards of modern popular journalism.

Mrs Beeton – one of only two studio portraits taken of her.

Far right
Samuel Beeton – a young radical of intense creative energy.

In an age of orderliness, when schoolchildren sang hymns in morning assembly praising work and high principles, *Beeton's Book of Household Management* summed up everything that Victorian middle-class life aspired to. God was in His Heaven, and the world was in its place. Men went forth to business, while women busied themselves at home organizing staff, supervising meals, attending the children and receiving calls. In a woman's world the daily round was dedicated to providing a haven of hot meals and velvet comfort for the master of the house returning from the office. She was not encouraged to discuss the issues of the day, to think independently or to develop any awareness of her true position in the Divine jig-saw.

She was expected not to have views, but 'accomplishments'. Middle-class family life was heavy with stuffed formality. Affection took the form of sentimentality, and passionate urges had no place in the home. Husbands could not see their wives as anything other than accessories to the family ideal. It was an age when an Englishman's home really was his castle – built like a fortress to shut out the harsh realities of the suffering outside.

Within it, women were corseted by convention. Intellectual interests were frowned upon and self-expression, beyond the piano and the embroidery frame, was unthinkable. The Brontë sisters, Emily, Anne and Charlotte,

A middle-class family at tea in the mid-Victorian era.

scribbling in the isolation of a Yorkshire parsonage, knew the pressures only too well. It was not considered 'delicate' for women to be writers and they quietly published their first books under the names Ellis, Acton and Currer Bell. Their devoted public were astonished to discover later that they were three young women.

The Victorian husband of means had a blinkered confidence that nothing could cloud his cosy, claustrophobic world – a view amply illustrated when the Marquis of Granby set his eye on a young married woman at a house party and she returned his interest. Later the Marquis slipped into her bedroom, and was on the point of waking her when her husband swept in. 'Hush!' begged the Marquis. 'Don't wake her. I was passing and I thought I smelt fire – but all is well.' The husband gratefully pumped his hand and thanked him warmly.

It is no surprise that the Victorians coined the expression Home Sweet Home and framed it in tapestry work over the humblest fireplace. Without the home's reassuring rules and principles life for thousands would have lost its lacing. Mrs Beeton was one of a new breed in the long march of history, and one of her most important achievements was to encourage women to seek an independent identity. For Mrs Beeton was not the dowdy old Victorian dragon that many believed. She was a young attractive woman with a sharp mind and a taste for social life and Parisian dresses. Like Florence Nightingale and Octavia Hill, she was a 'New Woman' who subtly changed the outlook of the age, and expanded women's horizons. Queen Victoria ranted against 'this mad, wicked folly of women's rights', but with the example of single-minded individuals like Isabella, nothing could stop the turning of the tide.

In the thirty years following Mrs Beeton's death but still in Victoria's reign, women had changed and a writer in the *Daily Graphic* could look back at the typical woman of Mrs Beeton's day:

> She was amiable, though rather timid, perhaps, and quite incapable of looking after herself. Hedged in with a thousand conventions, and a slave to as many unreasonable prejudices and traditions, her life was terribly cramped and confined. She rarely knew the luxury of having a will of her own, unless by chance she happened to marry a man somewhat weaker than herself. As for the young lady of today who, in our hours of ease, is the rival of man's athletic prowess, and when sickness wrings the brow is not only a devoted nurse but also a very skilful doctor, what need is there to describe her? Is not the whole difference between her and her grandmother shown and exemplified by their respective skirts?

THE REAL MRS BEETON

The Industrial Revolution had created a wealthy class who emulated the aristocracy and patronized the masses. The two-sided coin of money and misery became common currency throughout Victoria's reign.

Poor families laboured in back rooms making matchboxes, cutting cloth, hammering, forging, stamping and stitching products for the first consumer society. A fifth of the population lived in cellars, sanitary conditions in the towns were appalling and one-roomed houses were built without even a thought of drains. Lord Palmerston visited one such place and found four families living there, one in each corner. Many wandered around the country in search of wages, often moving lodgings every three weeks. By contrast, the new middle classes spent their wealth buying status and stability, and expressing it in cluttered decor and suffocating style.

In this sea of restless insecurity, the home became an island of stability – a monument to the rewards that hard work and Christian principles could bring. Mrs Beeton is acclaimed as its high-priestess, but she was rather more than that. Her formidable collection of 'tried and tested' recipes and her sound advice on hygiene, etiquette and family life were innovations. She introduced domestic science to the kitchen, and turned the whole idea of cookery books upside down. In much the same way that the corset gave Victorian women a new dimension and the belief that whalebone was a life-support, *Beeton's Book of Household Management* proved equally indispensible.

A growing army of women, hungry to expand their horizons, waited eagerly for Mrs Beeton's magazine columns. She wrote on travel, Paris fashions, cookery, women's interests and a wide range of lively topics which her capped and crinolined readers found irresistible. Here, at last, was someone like them; someone who understood their problems and shared their hopes and aspirations in elevating family life and wifely duty.

Household Management was originally published in monthly parts, and was crammed with recipes sent in by readers. It was claimed that all the recipes were tested by Mrs Beeton personally, although Fanny Craddock once worked out that she would have had to have been an octogenarian if she had! But even those probably tried by her cook were rigorously checked before publication. Indeed, it was perhaps because she was *not* a professional cook that Mrs Beeton approached her recipes with such intelligent care, tasting, listing and costing as she went. She addressed each dish with the thoroughness of one who could see the recipe from the reader's point of view, answering questions before they were asked without the assumptions and arrogance that might be acquired by a lifetime in the kitchen. Like all good journalists she was in touch with the mood of the time – and in many ways years ahead of it.

What Mrs Beeton's readers never realized was that the life of the woman

The gentle pursuits of the drawing room – papa enjoys pictures from the stereoscope with his wife and daughters.

they worshipped flew more in the face of convention than they could ever imagine. In an age when marriages were often little more than formal arrangements, hers was a passionate love-match.

At a period when a woman's place was firmly in the home, she travelled to work each day, pursuing her career with an independence which left male commuters puce behind their copies of *The Times*. Middle-class couples tended to marry late, after long courtships in which they prepared a solid financial foundation for home and family. Isabella Beeton married Sam – a thin man with creative energy and intense, electric eyes – when she was just twenty.

It was a partnership unlike any her readers might dream of experiencing. Isabella and Sam were lovers, friends and business partners who fired each other with ideas and a zest for life despite daunting hurdles of personal tragedy. As Victorian women of the merchant classes slavishly sought to become ideal wives in the only way they knew how – by pleasing their husbands and supervising the home, the engine-room of married life – Isabella and Sam Beeton lived as equal partners. He began as her mentor, guiding and encouraging her first uncertain writing efforts. She blossomed to become his inspiration, chief advisor, and business strategist – the meticulous genius on whom the immense success of their publishing adventures rested.

Then suddenly, at the height of her achievements as an individual and a pioneer of women's progress, Isabella died in childbirth from puerperal fever, having produced a healthy baby boy, Mayson. The infection was probably due to carelessness in hygiene by the doctor and nurse. Within a week of giving birth, at the age of twenty-eight, she was dead, leaving a heartbroken Sam and a host of pale immitators who tried unsuccessfully to capture her imagination and flair.

Mrs Beeton's Cookery Book is still considered the ideal wedding gift. It was read as pure escapism by men on Scott's Antarctic expedition and by hungry prisoners-of-war in the Singapore camps.

One hundred and fifty years on, the legacy of Mrs Beeton's shrewd practicality, wry sense of humour, sound kitchen sense and fine-tuning to the spirit of fellow-women from all walks of life, can be commonly found in magazines and cookery books everywhere. In many ways Mrs Beeton was ahead of her time. That history finally caught up with her is a tribute to her innovative talent.

2
At Home With Mrs Beeton

Isabella Beeton had been a housewife for five years when her indispensable kitchen bible, *Household Management*, was published. While the monthly partwork had been a pacesetter in magazine production, the book itself was an enormous success, selling 60,000 copies in the first year. It became a familiar sight on scrubbed kitchen shelves of the grandest middle- and upper-class houses.

Her own home, where most of the recipes were tested, approved and in some cases rejected, lay in the idyllic heart of that Victorian dreamland called suburbia. Isabella and Sam whiled away the long weeks of their engagement planning and fitting out their modest new semi-detached villa at 523 Uxbridge Road, Pinner. Nothing remains of it today – it suffered a direct hit in the Blitz. The site was later occupied by a filling station and, today, by a modern shopping parade.

On 10 July 1856, a glorious day when the Downs shimmered in the summer heat, they married in style at Epsom Racecourse where Isabella's stepfather, Henry Dorling, owned the Grandstand. Isabella's half-sister, Lucy Dorling, was a bridesmaid. As she recalled many years later: 'It was a gorgeous day, just after the summer meeting. How picturesque the guests looked out on the course in front – the big skirts and the fringed parasols.' Isabella, it was reported, wore 'a white silk dress, trimmed in little flowers from waist to hem, and a large white bouquet and veil.' Each tiered frill had been embroidered by a different sister.

Isabella and Sam left by carriage for a European tour, which was not quite as grand as it sounds. Sightseeing was crammed between business trips to printing houses and bookshops. The young couple, happy in each other's

Epsom and the Grandstand – Isabella's imposing childhood home.

company, tramped for miles across Paris to save on fares. Back at Pinner the house, with its pretentious facade, blooming rhododendrons and neatly-trimmed lawns, waited bright and clean for their return. Their wedding gifts, laid out for them, ranged from an old toast-rack from an ageing relative to a rather pompous white piano from Isabella's stepfather.

No. 2 Chandos Villas had a lobby leading into a roomy entrance hall. The dining room, where the Beetons entertained a large circle of relatives and a small circle of friends, was 16 feet square with a high ceiling. Adjoining it was a 17ft 6in drawing room, followed by what the builder called 'domestic offices' – a long extension housing a spacious kitchen and pantry. There was a small wine cellar, attic accommodation for the staff, five bedrooms and – something of a luxury – two lavatories.

Isabella was a firm believer in the value of hot baths (Sam preferred cold) and it is a measure of her single-mindedness that she insisted on a bathroom with hot and cold running water – a rarity in middle-class homes (and in any other homes, for that matter) but her convictions about cleanliness were total.

The original builder's sales brochure, wooing commuters to the cholera-free suburbs.
Far right
The price of healthy living – rent for Chandos Villas was £50 a year.
Facing page
Isabella insisted on a bathroom. This one is typical of the period though few middle-class homes had one.

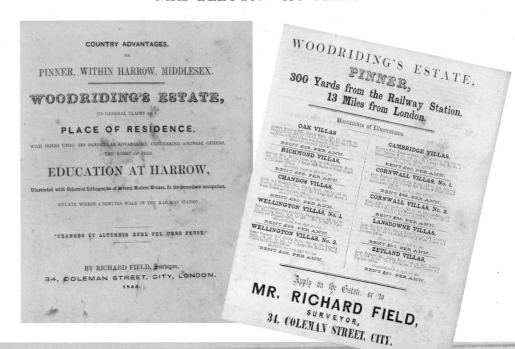

Sam and Isabella's home at No. 2 Chandos Villas. The architect attempted to transport the grandeur of Belgravia to rural Pinner.

CHANDOS VILLAS

To Seat Five Persons

Women were an unusual sight among the ranks of male commuters. Isabella caused a stir by travelling to the office daily.

Thackeray's description of 'the great unwashed' was no exaggeration. For 141 years there had been a tax on soap, and the London tallow boilers had plied a meagre trade. Three years before Isabella's wedding, Gladstone repealed the levy and quality soap for the masses became available. Pears stepped up their advertising ('Two years ago I used your soap – since when I have used no other') and the luxury of a bathroom began to exert its appeal. Isabella's reasons for insisting on one were entirely practical reasons – languishing in a bath would have been her idea of boredom – but 2 Chandos Villas must, nevertheless, have been the envy of the neighbours.

By modern suburban standards it was almost a mansion, but the Beetons had chosen one of the cheapest of eight pairs of adjoining semis which ran in a ribbon of red-brick symmetry down to the station. Its position had obviously influenced their decision – just thirteen miles from bustling Bouverie Street where Sam ran his expanding publishing business – with the added attraction of seven years' free commuter travel thrown in by the builder. The rent was £50 a year – just within the range of middle-class businessmen on salaries of between £300 and £500 a year. Nelson's daughter, Horatia Nelson Ward, and her two married sons William and Nelson, had bought three of the neighbouring houses. The others were quickly taken by a local builder, an estate manager and one of Mrs Nelson Ward's widowed friends.

The trim semis, set back from the road, were part of a development called Woodridings Estate. The builder, anxious to recoup his investment, had hired a copywriter to produce a ten-page brochure extolling the virtues of suburban life. As journalists themselves Sam and Isabella must have smiled at the gushing prose. Playing on the anxieties of prospective purchasers to the full, the writer, having inspected every grave in the local cemetery, reassured them: 'At Pinner, there has never been a case of cholera, for the health and longevity of the district is attested by the Parish Register and the Church Yard tombstones.'

It was a shrewd piece of salesmanship. The Thames at the time was little more than an open sewer, and overcrowding in the narrow thoroughfares around Cheapside's Milk Street, where both Isabella and Sam were born, was unbearable. The House of Commons hung sacking soaked in lime at the windows during the summer, and the courts at Westminster Hall had to be evacuated because of the stench from the Thames.

The first choice of all is a healthy location (bubbled the brochure, advising Londoners to seek the wide open spaces of Pinner). The soil has natural drainage, so that a natural tenacity is not injurious as are the light soils on a dead flat. There is a lightness, an exuberance of feeling felt by the dweller on the high level above the river which he who inhabits the level parts of London (not the actual foggy fen, or the marshy moor, but all places on a low level) never enjoys. A feeling perhaps due to the fact that the air is in reality lighter, or less dense, and therefore of a bracing quality.

Proximity to town is another advantage – I mean such a proximity as may be sufficient to enable a person to attend business at business hours, for to be too close to London is not to be desired.

Seclusion: where a man feels himself in the country, as the Poet says 'with Nature and with Nature's God'. Where he can speak to those he meets as acquaintances, if not friends, and does not as at London have a continual series of faces pass before him, familiar to him, yet unknown, and strange yet without the value of novelty.

In all these points – Healthiness, Situation, Good Society, First Rate Education, Proximity to Town and Seclusion – I believe that Pinner will be found to excel. In its immediate vicinity there are first-rate houses of different classes, suited to the varying means of London householders at moderate rates.

It was hardly the soft sell, and it was obviously effective. By the time Sam and Isabella had set up home in Chandos Villas, thirty of the fifty completed houses on the estate had been rented by commuters – barristers, surgeons, clerks in the Admiralty, the India Office and the War Office, according to the Census.

Chandos Villas were a stroll from Pinner station, now Hatch End, which the London to Birmingham Railway had opened in 1844. The company had business links with local speculative builders and in some cases offered thirteen years free first-class commuter travel – one ticket per household – to new home-buyers. No efforts were spared to encourage the mass migration to the suburbs. Most of the houses were modelled closely on those recently built in Swiss Cottage and St John's Wood, and aimed at attracting families who yearned for a fashionable property but lacked the means to afford a fashionable area.

The Beeton's, grand for rural Pinner, was constructed in the Italian style with features borrowed haphazardly from even grander homes in Bayswater and Belgravia. They had water pumped from an artesian well by a faintly-thumping steam engine concealed on the estate. The villas, like most Victorian homes, had coal fires with supplies delivered weekly from a depot at Harrow station. Instead of open fires, Isabella had stoves fitted as they were less sooty and easier to keep clean.

Services were almost as good as the brochure promised. The post promised to arrive promptly at 8 a.m., before the morning exodus to the station began, and struggled to succeed. There was milk from herds of dairy cows which grazed across the road at Woodridings Farm, and butter and cheese were made in the village. Other food was bought from traders who called at the back door with fresh fruit and vegetables from Bushey, Watford and Edgware. Mrs Beeton later advised her readers in a section of *Household Management* headed 'Successful Marketing':

A daily supply is a daily waste. The running to and from the street door to the chandler's shop; the purchase of an ounce of this thing, or a quarter of a pound of that, is an error. Your grocery should be obtained regularly in quantities from respectable traders; potatoes should come in a sack . . . apples by the bushel . . . and not only may you have many pleasant additions to your dinner table by adopting a system of wholesale purchase, but you will upon the whole have more and pay less; be free of the worry of sending out continually for small supplies, and have at hand a stock to meet emergencies.'

Most houses could afford two or three staff; only six on the whole estate had just one servant. The Beeton's had three: a housemaid, a cook and later a nurse for baby Samuel Orchart who was to die in infancy. There was a gardener, too, who was immediately put to work by the new Mrs Beeton. She hated the red-brick frontage and called on all his expertise to screen it. Before the wedding distance had made it difficult for Isabella, living at Epsom with her family, to supervise setting up house. Sam would travel to Pinner by train and stay overnight to keep an eye on things. Then, back at his desk, he would write lengthy progress reports to his bride-to-be. For someone unaccustomed to matters normally attended to then by ladies, this was not easy. As the weeks before their wedding ticked away Sam, happy but harrassed, wrote:

I had excessively interesting interviews with the band of Pinner tradesmen and handcraftsmen. Your bricklayer commences making the place a mess on Tuesday, your carpenter commences his cupboard on the same day, and your painter follows them up closely at the end of the week.

Mr. Cutbush, the nurseryman, is going to run down tomorrow afternoon to see what shrubs, creepers, etc are the best to plant.

I have to go to choose the chimney piece tomorrow – I do heartily wish you were here to go with me – I've no doubt I shall make a terrible mess over this and other matters. What colour are your Venetian blinds to be? Green or Drab? They will have to be made, I apprehend. Do your parents know any good man?

Our bachelor bedroom is quite empty. The bed and bedstead are capital and the chest of drawers complete, with toilet cover, and my old buffalo rug before the fireplace and a washing stand – borrowed from Mrs. Scott – constitute the furniture. I had forgotten the sheet nailed to the window, so as not to expose us too much to the neighbours.

We took down coffee and sugar and sausages and had a good tea last night, and a first-rate breakfast this morning. We went last night to Pinner village, which was quite in commotion, being Saturday – I really believe I saw ten people altogether. The butcher's shop near the church was drawing a tremendous trade, and vice versa this morning the church was doing all the business.

As you truly said I didn't know what I had to do, and I certainly didn't. For what with pots and potatoes and gravel and carpets and crockery and creepers, grates and greens, fenders and scrapers and other hims and hers it certainly keeps a fellow well up to the mark.

Like all their letters it was written in a breezy yet intimate style, quite a contrast to the rather starched social formality of the day. For a couple who were to advise the readers of their *Englishwoman's Domestic Magazine* on the niceties of etiquette and letter-writing, their own notes to each other have a close, chatty flavour, more familiar today than in Victoria's time. On occasions Sam's letters came so thick and fast from the office that Isabella had to beg him not to send them in *Boy's Own Magazine* envelopes, as her stepfather was beginning to make comments. Henceforth they were despatched under plain wrapper. Running a busy publishing office, preparing for his wedding day and supervising workmen clearly gave poor Sam little free time, but he never forgot the precious progress reports on Pinner.

Isabella, a practical and decisive young woman, must have felt frustrated and often a little low in spirits at having to plan her first home by proxy. Sam kept up her enthusiasm and tempered her concern with humour. Soon he was able to report:

> The carpenter has finished your cupboard in the passage, and it's a grand place – there'll be room for four people to sleep if we're hard up for beds. The nice fresh smell of the wholesome paint, as you observed in a portion of your letter, still obtains as much as ever, only more so. I am told this will gradually increase until a healthy climax is reached. I can only add I'm exceedingly grateful.

Their exchange of letters before the wedding reveals a touching case of the butterflies as the day drew nearer. Isabella's family, while not hostile to Sam, did not entirely approve. He was impulsive and creative, and depended on a profession which, however respectable, required him to live on his wits and gamble on the fickleness of fashion. But theirs was an affair of the heart and, although there was some private concern for Isabella, they were clearly in love, as their letters show, and it would have taken a runaway train to stop them.

Pinner
Sunday Eveng.

My beloved Bella,

I have been wandering through the fields, full of the newly cut hay, for the last hour or so, and have returned perfectly envious and full of bile – for I can assure you that I was the only unhappy mortal who was alone. I met many happy maidens with many happy men . . . there was always somebody with somebody else, so to this fact do you owe, my dearest, this letter, as I have made up my mind to be even with the people I have seen in some way or another, and if they are *with* those they love they cannot at any rate be experiencing this pleasure now felt by me of writing to her, 'in whose hands are all the corners of my heart'.

You must have had a lovely day at Brighton, for it has been charmingly sunshiny – the moon is electrotyping at this moment with its beautiful silvery light all around, and I instinctively am walking with you on Brighton Pier, and almost hear you ejaculate 'Oh! Sam, if only you knew.' I don't know why it is, Bella mia, but you never get any further than that.

Now, down to earth again, and let furniture act on us as attention! on a regiment on parade. What colour are the cord tassles to be? These blinds, oh these blinds, I can't get along with them at all. The plumber and the carpenter have departed the house at last – peace go with them! – pieces they've left behind. The rooms are all cleaned – the stoves polished – I took the brushes down – quite ready for carpets and blinds, and all the rest of your property. I have written a note to your friend Mr. Green that he can send down the food for Chandos as soon as he pleases, as it's quite ready to be lined.

Been manipulating severely any people today, Bella! Have Father and Mamma been using you today as of old monarchs used the man who stood behind their chair, oranmented with cap and bells – to wit – trot him out, and then laugh at his stepping. I hope not . . .

Bella dearest, three Sundays more and then the holidays, as the school phrase has it. None can tell how grateful I feel and am to the 'Great Good.' May He bless and protect you, my own dearest one, and make us happy and contented in each other's true and ardent love.

Je t'embrasse de tout mon coeur.

Yours, in all things,

S. O. Beeton.

Epsom
June 22nd 1856

My own darling Sam,

You cannot imagine how grateful I felt this morning when I received your note telling me you were so much better, and although some parts of the letter were a little bit unkind and cool, that small sentence quite made up for everything sharp, although I have no doubt you did not mean it to be so. You have written me so very many loving letters lately that if I receive only one or two pages, and those pages very matter-of-fact, I imagine you are cross with me and don't care so much about me.

Now you are better I am going to ask you a question about the rest of the furniture. I did not like to ask you on Wednesday evening as you seemed so poorly. When shall I come to finish because, as you well know, there are several things to do yet? You can write and let me know what time will suit you best.

During church time this morning, instead of listening to the sound of the Gospel and profiting thereby, I have been giving my imagination full play. I have been thinking how nice it will be at Pinner with the only being I at this moment care for on earth; how kind you will be to poor little me, and how you will say sometimes, 'I don't think I shall go to town this morning but stay and have a quiet day in the country.' You will arrange matters so, won't you dear? I am so very sorry you are not here today. I seem quite lost without you now.

Don't you think I shall have a great deal to answer for, I mean thinking so much about you; always saying to myself, I wonder what Sam is doing and what he is thinking about etc., etc. The time is fast approaching, my precious pet, for our affair. God grant that nothing may happen now to prevent our union, may he give you health and strength to enjoy many years of happiness with my heart's best love,

Believe me, darling Sam,

Yours with all love's devotion,

Bella Mayson

Your Uncle Tom has written to say he shall be happy to come on the 8th of July instead of the 10th. The next time you see him just inform him of his mistake, as it would be rather funny to come two days before the Fair.

Oh Sam, if only you knew.

In sharp contrast to the heavy opulence upstairs, Victorian kitchens were functional affairs, rich in appetizing smells and clouds of rising steam. By our standards cooking methods were extremely basic, relying on experience, touch and tastebuds. There was, of course, no split-level thermostatic precision but, in the right hands, meals emerged as perfect as any from a hi-tech kitchen of today, and possibly tastier. However, it was the age of invention, and gadgets of all kinds were universally popular.

Mrs Beeton's letters, still in the possession of the family, throw little light on her own kitchen which she appears to have fitted with the same attention to detail as the rest of the house. She even posted Sam a crayon sketch of how the cupboard shelves in the cellar were to be arranged. When he reported that the kitchen had been painted and the grate fixed – 'so as to be useful in case of much fire being required for our "petit-diners"' – they arranged to meet in town for the mammoth task of buying the utensils. Sam wisely did not volunteer to put this on his list of single-handed jobs. A month before the wedding he offered to meet Isabella and her mother and take them to choose kitchen equipment, along with a bed and some furniture.

Gas cookers were in their infancy at the time. In 1834 a prototype was purchased by the Bath Hotel in Leamington where a celebration dinner was

Below-stairs staff at work. This kitchen would have been similar in many ways to Mrs Beeton's where the recipes were carefully tried and tested.

THE LEAMINGTON STOVE, OR KITCHENER.

Mrs Beeton's most likely choice of kitchen range for Chandos Villas – the Improved Leamington.

Cast iron kitchen ranges, which had many uses from cooking to general heating, were an essential part of below-stairs equipment

cooked for a hundred guests. 'Everything was excellently done,' one diner reported, 'and notwithstanding that the fish, pudding, fowl, bacon and greens had been steamed in the same steamer, no dish had contracted any unpleasant taste from its neighbour.'

John Sharp, the inventor, was surprised to open his door in Northampton to find Earl Spencer descending from a carriage, flanked by an escort of four gold-braided riders. He strode inside and asked if he might have a gas-cooked meal. As a result, the first factory opened in the year Isabella was born. Roasting ovens had not been properly developed – joints of meat were hung, either from the ceiling or inside a tall cabinet, over naked gas jets.

By the time *Household Management* was published they were becoming increasingly popular, though Mrs Beeton, something of a traditionalist in cooking matters, had her reservations: 'Gas cooking can scarcely now be considered a novelty,' she wrote, and continued:

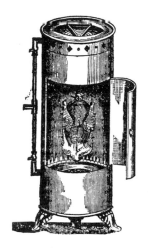

An early gas oven – Mrs Beeton was not entirely impressed with the efficiency of such ovens.

Many establishments both small and large have been fitted with apparatus for cooking in this mode, which undoubtedly exhibits some advantages. Thus the heat may be more regularly supplied to the substance cooking, and the operation is essentially a clean one, because there can be no cinders or other dirt to be provided for. Some labour and attention necessary, too, with a coal fire or close stove, may be saved; and beside this it may perhaps be said that culinary operations are reduced, by this means, to something like a certainty.

There are, however, we think many objections to this mode of cooking, more especially when applied to small domestic establishments. For instance, the ingenious machinery necessary for carrying it out requires cooks perfectly conversant with its use; and if the gas, when the cooking operations are finished, be not turned off there will be a large increase in the cost of cooking, instead of the economy which it has been supposed to bring. For large establishments, such as some of the immense London warehouses where a large number of young men have to be catered for daily, it may be well adapted, as it is just possible that a slight increase in the supply of gas necessary for a couple of joints may serve equally to cook a dozen dishes.

Isabella finally chose a coal-fired stove for herself. She approved of hot-plates, which were a recent development and enabled several dishes to be prepared at the same time. They were ideal too, she noted, for slow braising and stewing as the meat became more tender and the gravy less reduced.

It is almost certain that, after shopping around, Isabella chose the Improved Leamington Kitchener. Models ranged from £5 15s. to £23 10s at Slack's in the Strand. In the first edition of *Household Management* she reviews three kitchen stoves, but writes with such familiarity and praise about the Leamington that one cannot help but assume it was from personal experience. She enthused:

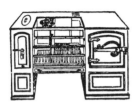

It is said to surpass any other range in use, for easy cooking by one fire. It has a hot plate which is well-calculated for an ironing stove, and on which as many vessels as will stand upon it may be kept boiling without being either soiled or injured. Besides, it has a perfectly ventilated and spacious wrought-iron roaster, with moveable shelves, draw-out stand, double dripping-pan and meat stand.

The roaster can be converted into an oven by closing the valves, when bread and pastry can be baked in it in a superior manner. It also has a large iron boiler with brass tap and steam pipe, round and square gridirons for chops and steaks, ash-pan, open fire for roasting, and a set of ornamental coverings with plate-warmer attached.

New kitchen ranges were displayed in all the best stores. This model, illustrated in Household Management, *had Mrs Beeton's cautious approval, but fell short of the Leamington's standards.*

The Leamington took first prize at the 1851 Great Exhibition and sales, enhanced by the glowing prose of Mrs Beeton, presumably delighted the manufacturers.

Kitchen ranges at the time tended to be the size of a small locomotive and required almost as much fuel and maintenance. They were marvellously efficient and coped effortlessly with the heavy catering indulged in in larger houses, but the poor kitchen maid must have cursed them. Scuttles of coal had to be hauled from the coal-hole to keep the hungry fire burning and, at the end of each day, the stove had to be stripped down and scrubbed ready for breakfast next morning.

Mrs Beeton, a great admirer of Florence Nightingale whose principles of basic hygiene had drastically reduced Crimean death-tolls, was a stickler for cleanliness. At Chandos Villas she could afford only one housemaid, but the girl charged with the daunting task of meeting her exacting standards must have sunk into exhausted sleep at the end of each day. While Sam was a radical with a desire to change the order of things, Mrs Beeton had no such social or political mission. Her crusade was to improve domestic conditions by elevating standards from the drawing-room down to the kitchen. Upstairs such elevation was to be attained through orderliness, economy, compassion and the social graces. Downstairs it could be achieved only with the heavy artillery of scrubbing brushes, polish, mops and mousetraps.

The mistress of the house juggled with time and motion study, personnel management and the problems of putting her home on a critical path analysis with all the dignity she could muster. As the influence of Mrs Beeton's gospel of domestic science spread, many houses must have resembled a food factory run by a detachment of the Coldstream Guards. She worked out in great detail household duties which interlocked and overlapped with military precision, and provided work-schedules for houses of every size and permutation of staff.

Isabella spent hours in Pinner drawing up timetables of duties, working methods which left nothing to the imagination, lists of utensils and tidy-boxes to keep them in. The mistress, far from languidly overseeing this swarm of activity from the comfort of a chaise-longue, was required to be up at the crack of dawn helping staff where necessary, issuing orders and superintending the buying, cooking, cleaning, making and mending. It was small wonder that the prolific Isabella and Sam chose as the Beeton's publishing logo the sign of a beehive.

The good mistress's biblical standards were set by Proverbs XXXI: 25–28: 'Strength and honour are her clothing, and she shall rejoice in time to come. She openeth her mouth with wisdom, and in her tongue is the law of kindness. She looketh well to the ways of her household, and eateth not the bread of idleness. Her children arise up and call her blessed; her husband also and he praiseth her.' Mrs Beeton certainly knew how to get the message home.

Soon after her marriage she began translating French novels for Sam's *Englishwoman's Domestic Magazine*. Within eight months she was writing cookery and household columns, and it must have become increasingly necessary to work out an efficient programme which combined journalism with household duties. The system she evolved possibly formed the basis for the detailed advice in *Household Management*. An interesting little section, aimed at homes with only one housemaid, might well have been the picture of daily life at Pinner while Sam was away at the office.

The maid-of-all-work's day began by lighting the fires about 5 a.m. and preparing the dining-room for breakfast. Next came dusting, shaking mats, sweeping and cleaning the brasses. After breakfast she had to wash the dishes,

make the beds, clean the bedrooms and the rest of the house. Then it was down to help cook prepare lunch, lay the table, serve the meal and clear away afterwards. The afternoon may have been spent attending to dirty jobs in the scullery, such as cleaning knives or boots and shoes. By then it was on without break to the ritual of tea-time, turning down the beds, preparing for the evening meal and cleaning up after it. 'A bustling and active girl,' Mrs Beeton optimistically believed, 'will always find time to do a little needlework for herself, if she lives with consistent and reliable people.'

Isabella saw the kitchen as 'the great laboratory of every household' and, as a recently-married housewife herself, was in a good position to make helpful suggestions on its design and arrangement. She had five guiding principles on the location of a kitchen in a new house:

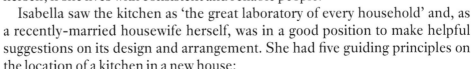

1: Convenience of distribution in its parts, with largeness and dimension. 2: Excellence of light, height of ceiling and good ventilation. 3: Easiness of access, without passing through the house. 4: Sufficiently remote from the principle appartments of the house that the members, visitors or guests of the family may not perceive the odour incident to cooking, or hear the noise of culinary operations. 5: Plenty of fuel and water which, with the scullery, pantry and storeroom, should be so near it as to offer the smallest possible trouble in reaching them.

Not everyone, of course, could have a kitchen built to their requirements, but any advice was considered valuable. Most Victorian middle-class women, though skilled in the delicate arts of the drawing-room, were totally unprepared for the duties of marriage. After the lavish wedding, and equally sumptuous reception, many a bride must have felt lost and ineffectual when her husband had gone to business. For someone out of their depth, Mrs Beeton was a godsend. In her all embracing book of advice no detail was overlooked and no assumptions ever made. Perhaps drawing from her own experience on that shopping trip with Sam and her mother, she even supplied a list of basic utensils for the new kitchen:

Victorian kitchen staff required a thorough knowledge of the formidable array of utensils stocked in the average middle-class household.

		s.	d.
1	Tea-kettle	6s.	6d
1	Toasting fork	1	0
1	Bread grater	1	0
1	Pair Brass Candlesticks	3	6
1	Teapot and Tray	6	6
1	Bottle-jack	9	6
6	Spoons	1	6
2	Candlesticks	2	6
1	Candle box	1	4
6	Knives and Forks	5	3
2	Sets of Skewers	1	0
1	Meat Chopper	1	9
1	Cinder-sifter	1	3
1	Coffee Pot	2	3
1	Colander	1	6
3	Block-tin Saucepans	5	9
5	Iron Saucepans	12	0
1	Ditto and Steamer	6	6
1	Large Boiling Pot	10	0
4	Iron Stewpans	8	9
1	Dripping-pan and Stand	6	6
1	Dustpan	1	0
1	Fish and Egg Slice	1	9
2	Fish Kettles	10	0
1	Flour Box	1	0
3	Flat-irons	3	6
2	Frying Pans	4	0
1	Grid-iron	2	0
1	Mustard Pot	1	0
1	Salt Cellar	0	8
1	Pepper Box	0	6
1	Pair of Bellows	2	0
3	Jelly Moulds	8	0
1	Plate Basket	5	6
1	Cheese Toaster	1	10
1	Coal Shovel	2	6
1	Wood Meat-screen	30	0
	The Set £8	11	1

It was essential, as with everything in the gleaming Beeton kitchen, to keep utensils scrupulously clean:

As not only health but life may be said to depend on the cleanliness of culinary utensils, great attention must be paid to their condition generally, but more especially that of saucepans, stew-pans and boilers. Inside they should be kept perfectly clean and, where an open fire is used, the outside as clean as possible. Soup-pots and kettles should be washed immediately after being used, and dried before the fire.

The 'domestic offices' described by Mrs Beeton's builder's sales brochure would have included a cool pantry for storing food and a scullery for washing pots and pans, leaving the kitchen as free as possible for cooking. As many kitchens were below-stairs, the dim nooks and corners were often brightened with whitewash. Mrs Beeton preferred tiles, which could easily be wiped clean and – in the days before linoleum – a wooden or stone floor which could be robustly scrubbed.

Sam, needless to say, had a hot dinner waiting however late he returned from the city, even on the occasions when he missed the last train and walked the thirteen miles home. It was, by all accounts, a happy, well-run house. But as Isabella became more involved in collecting, testing and writing the recipes which went into her half-million-word masterpiece, the kitchen at Pinner became the nerve-centre of their most successful project in publishing.

3
Commanders in Crinolines
The Mistress of the House

The Victorian age saw the dawn of many changes, but perhaps none so fundamental and lasting as the emergence of 'the New Woman'. Family life towards the middle of the nineteenth century, when Mrs Beeton was a girl, revolved almost entirely around double standards. Women were caught in a vice of drawing-room hypocracy. On the one hand, they were expected to be selfless, skilled in all the social arts, cloistered and completely ignorant of the world outside. On the other, they had to organize the house, the servants and the meals, balance their accounts, look after the children and be vaguely involved in 'good works'.

Women were not educated for any of these heavy responsibilities, however. Ironically the Board Schools began teaching homecraft to working-class girls, but the children of wealthy parents at 'ladies' colleges' received little more than a grounding in the classics. In the main, education for middle-class girls was merely a diversion to while away the time until they married. They picked up a smattering of languages, the ability to play a few well-worn pieces on the piano, a little painting and a lot of needlework. Mrs Beeton, who was luckier than most, attended a reputable finishing school in Heidelberg.

Generally the role of mistress of the house, towards which young women irrevocably moved, was completely neglected in their education. Womanhood was somehow assumed to be achieved by natural means, with the skills of motherhood and domestic arrangement being picked up on the way. The problems and anxieties incurred on the rose-strewn path to married bliss were of no interest to the husband. He expected his bride to run the house and preferred not to hear of her failures.

It was fashionable to have an industrious wife, but all her efforts had to be

208   PUNCH, OR THE LONDON CHARIVARI.   [November 21, 1863.

SERVANTGALISM.

Mary. "Did you call, Mum?"

Lady. "Yes, Mary! I thought I told you not to wear your Hoop before you had done your Rooms, because you broke the Jugs and Basins with it!"

Mary. "Oh, Mum! You see the *Sweeps* were coming this Morning, and, really, I could not think of opening the Door to them such a Figger as I should ha' been without my Crinoline!"

concealed from her hard-working husband. Even the children were sometimes banished to the nursery to make life more comfortable for him. At the end of the day, with the meal prepared for his return eaten, the master's wife was expected to provide him with sympathetic companionship, no matter how difficult her own day had been. From breakfast to bed – and often especially bed – women were meant to endure, not enjoy.

Behind this rather oppressive attitude lay the Victorian notion that the home was more than bricks and mortar and juggling the books: it represented an outward show of moral standards and respectability, perhaps the most important social yardstick of the times. Wealth was important, but without the added weight of taste and high morality, was almost worthless. There were, too, countless women married to the *nouveau riche* of Bradford, Leeds and Manchester who found themselves thrust into grand surroundings without an inkling of the finesse required to carry off their new-found status with conviction.

Mrs Beeton could not have produced *Household Management* at a more propitious time. The boredom faced by middle-class women in the earlier part

Coping with the servants was a new problem for the young housewife and mother.

SUNDAY OUT.

Betsy :— "SHALL YOU BE A-GOIN' OUT THIS A'TERNOON, MEM?'
Mistress :— "I THINK NOT, BETSY."
Betsy :— "'COS YER CAN IF YER LIKE, *I* DON'T WANT TO GO OUT."

A new addition to the family reinforced the Victorian ideal of domestic values, though fathers were often clearly bored by the whole affair.

of the century was beginning to give way to a restless drive to become more involved in practical matters. A high degree of skill and accomplishment at anything was frowned upon – professionalism veered dangerously towards the question of a career. It was far less troublesome to be an amateur needlewoman, pianist or painter and wisely avoid whispered talk. For those women caught in the dilemma of comfortable living, Mrs Beeton proved a single-minded champion of their plight.

She saw the way to salvation through good plain food and a thorough knowledge of domestic affairs, passing on her instructions in a way which

Arranging the household duties was one of the mistress's first tasks of the day.

encouraged women to explore many venues in the cause of home and family which they might never have considered otherwise. By lacing her wisdom with historical anecdotes, classical notes and wry observations on men, she made *Household Management* an enduring best-seller. Far in advance of its times it also contained legal guidelines for women on divorce and on assault by their husbands.

Readers must have been gratified to discover that Isabella's ideal mistress was not without intelligence, humour and compassion. Her strict rules and schedules provided relief and security for the beleaguered housewife, rather

Sewing was considered to be one of the feminine arts. Sam and Isabella took it further by selling fashion patterns for the latest clothes. Women, they rightly guessed, would be eager to try them out.

than impossible standards to live up to. In a country still recovering from the grimness of the Crimean War Mrs Beeton's analogy of the mistress of the house resembling the commander of an army was both topical and appealing. Generals were the celebrities of the day, and the orderliness and discipline evoked in the 'Role Of The Mistress' in *Household Management* mirrored Victorian ideals:

THE MISTRESS

As with the commander of an army, or the leader of any enterprise, so it is with the mistress of any house. Her spirit will be seen through the whole establishment; and in just proportion as she performs her duties intelligently and thoroughly, so will her domestics follow her path. Of all those acquirements, which more particularly belong to the feminine character, there are none which take the higher rank in our estimation than such as enter into a knowledge of household duties; for on these are perpetually dependent the happiness, comfort and well-being of a family.

In this opinion we are borne out by the author of *The Vicar Of Wakefield*, who says: 'The modest virgin, the prudent wife, and the careful matron are much more serviceable in life than petticoated philosophers, blustering heroines or virago queens. She who makes her husband and her children happy, who reclaims the one from vice and trains up the other to virtue, is a much greater character than ladies described in romances, whose whole occupation is to murder mankind with shafts from their quiver, or their eyes.'

Pursuing this picture, we may add, that to be a good housewife does not necessarily imply an abandonment of proper pleasures or amusing recreations; and we think it the more necessary to express this, as the performance of the duties of a mistress may to some minds seem to be incompatible with the enjoyment of life. Let us, however, now proceed to describe some of those home qualities and virtues which are necessary to the proper management of a Household, and then point out the plan which may be the most profitably pursued for the daily regulation of its affairs.

Early rising is one of the most essential qualities which enter into good Household Management, as it is not only the parent of health, but of innumerable other advantages. Indeed, when a mistress is an early riser, it is almost certain that her house will be orderly and well-managed. On the contrary, if she remain in bed till a late hour then the domestics who, as we have observed, invariably partake somewhat of their mistress's character, will surely become sluggards. To self-indulgence all are more or less disposed, and it is not to be expected that servants are freer from this fault than the heads of houses. The great Lord Chatham thus gave his advice in reference to this subject: 'I would have inscribed on the curtains of your bed and the walls of your chamber, "If you do not rise early, you can make progress in nothing".'

Cleanliness is also indispensable to health, and must be studied both in regard to the person and the house, and all that it contains. Cold or tepid baths should be employed every morning unless, on account of illness or other circumstances, they should be deemed objectionable.

Frugality and economy are home virtues, without which no household can prosper. Dr Johnson says: 'Frugality may be termed the daughter of Prudence, the sister of Temperance, and the parent of Liberty. He that is extravagant will quickly become poor, and poverty will enforce dependence and invite corruption.' The necessity of practising economy should be evident to everyone, whether in the possession of an income no more than sufficient for a family's requirements, or of a large fortune which puts financial adversity out of the question. We must always remember that it is a great merit in housekeeping to manage a little well. 'He is a good waggoner,' says Bishop Hall, 'that can turn in a little room. To live well in abundance is the praise of the estate, not of the person. I will study more how to give a good account of my little, than how to make it more.' In this there is true wisdom and, it may be added, that those who can manage a little well are most likely to succeed in their management of large matters. Economy and frugality must never, however, be allowed to degenerate into parsimony and meanness.

For many ladies, the tea shop was often the fulcrum of social life outside the home. Young retainers, up from the country on their first season, are overawed by the goods on display. Senior staff, waiting to escort the ladies home, have clearly seen it all before.

Despite Isabella's firm belief in these rather spartan methods (her only private reservation was the cold baths she strongly advocated) she was conscious of the inner feelings of her 'sisters'. After the preparation and tensions which preceded any wedding there was, and still is, an inevitable sense of anti-climax when the husband is away at work, and the new bride left alone in a new house in a strange neighbourhood. Boredom and lack of purpose at Pinner had originally given her the urge to write. When she passed on her advice on good housekeeping the memories of her own experiences were obviously still vivid.

Women in these circumstances faced the additional problems of making new friends and buying clothes for social calls. In Mrs Beeton's day middle-class women, unlike their working-class counterparts, had no opportunity to bump into neighbours at the corner shop. There were no telephones to keep in touch with family and friends. Social calls were of immense importance, even though conducted with formality. Behind the iron gates and neat lawns of the new suburbs social constrictions made family life very insular. While living in a rural idyll was a welcome relief from the city, meeting other women and acquiring a sense of community was quite a struggle. Nevertheless, it had to be approached with caution:

The choice of acquaintances is very important to the happiness of a mistress and her family. A gossiping acquaintance who indulges in the scandal and ridicule of her neighbours, should be avoided as a pestilence. It is likewise all-necessary to beware, as Thomson sings:

> The whisper'd tale,
> That, like the fabling Nile, no fountain knows; – Fair-faced Deceit whose wily, conscious eye
> Ne'er looks direct; the tongue that licks the dust
> But, when it safely dares, as prompt to sting.

If the duties of a family do not sufficiently occupy the time of a mistress, society should be formed of such a kind as will tend to the mutual interchange of general and interesting information.

Friendships should not be hastily formed, nor the heart given at once to every newcomer. There are ladies who uniformly smile at, and approve everything and everybody, and who possess neither the courage to reprehend vice, nor the generous warmth to defend virtue. The friendship of such pesons is without attachment, and their love without affection or even preference. They imagine that anyone who has any penetration is ill-natured, and look coldly on a discriminating judgement.

It should be remembered, however, that this discernment does not always proceed from an uncharitable temper, but those who possess a long experience and thorough knowledge of the world scrutinize the conduct and dispositions of people before they trust themselves to the first fair appearances. Addison, who was not deficient in a knowledge of mankind, observes that 'a friendship which makes the least noise is very often the most useful; for which reason I should prefer a prudent friend to a zealous one.' And Joanna Baillie tells us that

> Friendship is no plant of hasty growth,
> Though planted in esteem's deep-fixed soil,
> The gradual culture of kind intercourse
> Must bring it to perfection.

Bad news from the kitchen could test the nerve of even the most accomplished hostess.

Hospitality is a most excellent virtue, but care has to be taken that the love of company for its own sake does not become a prevailing passion, for then the habit is no longer hospitality, but dissipation. Reality and truthfulness in this, as in all other duties of life, are the points to be studied for, as Washington Irving well says: 'There is an emanation from the heart in genuine hospitality which cannot be described, but is immediately felt, and puts the stranger at once at his ease.' With respect to the continuance of friendships, however, it may be found necessary in some cases for a mistress to relinquish, on assuming the responsibility of a household, many of those commenced in the earlier part of her life. This will be the more requisite if the number still retained be quite equal to her means and opportunities.

In conversation trifling occurrences, such as small disappointments, petty annoyances and other everyday incidents should never be mentioned to your friends. The extreme injudiciousness of repeating these will be at once apparent when we reflect on the unsatisfactory discussions which they too frequently occasion, and on the load of advice which they are the cause of being tendered, and which is too often of a kind neither to be useful nor agreeable.

Greater events, whether of joy or sorrow, should be communicated to friends; and, on such occasions, their sympathy gratifies and comforts. If the mistress be a wife, never let an account of her husband's failings pass her lips; and in cultivating the power of conversation, she should keep the versified advice of Cowper continually in her memory, that it

Should flow like water after summer showers,
Nor as if raised by mere mechanic powers.

In reference to its style, Dr. Johnson who was himself greatly distinguished for his colloquial abilities, says that 'no style is more extensively acceptable than the narrative, because this does not carry an air of superiority over the rest of the company, and therefore is most likely to please them. For this purpose we should store our memory with short anecdotes and entertaining pieces of history. Almost everyone listens with eagerness to contemporary history.' Vanity often co-operates with curiosity, for he that is a hearer in one place wishes to qualify himself to be a principal speaker in some inferior company, and therefore no more attention is given to narrations than anything else in conversation. It is true indeed that sallies of wit and quick replies are very pleasing in conversation, but they frequently tend to raise envy in some of the company.

Good temper should be cultivated by every mistress, as upon it the welfare of the household may be said to turn. Indeed its influence can hardly be over-estimated, as it has the effect of moulding the characters of those around her, and of acting most beneficially on the happiness of the domestic circle. Every head of a household should strive to be cheerful, and should never fail to show a deep interest in all that appertains to the being of those who claim the protection of her roof. Gentleness, not partial and temporary but universal and regular, should pervade her conduct, for where such a spirit is habitually manifested, it not only delights her children, but makes her domestics attentive and respectful; her visitors are also pleased by it, and their happiness is increased.

Clothes were, of course, an important topic for women of the era, and Mrs Beeton had already attracted a loyal readership in her column in the *Englishwoman's Domestic Magazine*. The first department stores – Bainbridge's in Newcastle, and Kendal Milne in Manchester – had opened in 1850 to sell clothing. William Whiteley's in Bayswater, launched in 1863, the year of the second edition of *Household Management*, branched into jewellery, but they were very much in their infancy. Whiteley's, for example, had a staff of only three. Women of means had their dresses tailored in thousands of small silk mercers and dressmakers' shops which were growing in number each year. Mrs Beeton, who travelled to Paris to choose the colour fashion plates for the journal, had a strong eye for design, tempered always with her ever-practical approach. 'What can be more disagreeable,' she wrote in a typical piece, 'than to see a lady's rich silk skirt sweeping the streets as she walks? It is extravagant, inelegant and extremely dirty.' The famous studio daguerreotype of Isabella, which hung in the National Portrait Gallery, showed her wearing a dress she had had made up from a bolt of striped red silk, the gift from a racehorse owner at Epsom. Her ankles are discreetly out of camera, but it is highly unlikely that the skirt swept the floor. Isabella's fashion articles were written anonymously, but readers of *Household Management* must have sensed, nevertheless, the voice of authority:

On the important subject of dress and fashion we cannot do better than quote an opinion from the eighth volume of the *Englishwoman's Domestic Magazine*. The writer there [*Mrs Beeton herself*] says: 'Let people write, talk, lecture, satirize as they may, it cannot be denied that whatever is the prevailing mode in attire, let it intrinsically be ever so absurd, it will never look as ridiculous as another, or as any other which, however convenient, comfortable or even becoming, is totally opposite in style to that generally worn.

Right: *Arranging a formal dinner was a major ordeal for any new wife. Dressing for it could be even more fraught with anxiety.*

———————

In purchasing articles of wearing apparel, whether it be a silk dress, a bonnet, shawl or riband, it is well for the buyer to consider three things: 1. That it be not too expensive for her purse. 2. That its colour harmonize with her complexion, and its size and pattern with her figure. 3. That its tint allow of its being worn with the other garments she possesses. The quaint Fuller observes that the good wife is none of our dainty dames, who love to appear in a variety of suits every day new, as if a gown like a stratagem in war were to be used but once. But our good wife sets up a sail according to the keel of her husband's estate; and, if of high parentage, she doth not so remember what she was by birth, that she forgets what she is by match.

To brunettes, or those ladies having dark complexions, silks of a grave hue are adapted. For blondes, or those having fair complexions, lighter colours are preferable, as the richer, deeper hues are too overpowering for the latter. The colours which go best together are green with violet; gold-colour with dark crimson or lilac; pale blue with scarlet; pink with black or white; and grey with scarlet or pink. A cold colour generally requires a warm tint to give life to it. Grey and pale blue, for instance, do not combine well, both being cold colours.

The dress of the mistress should always be adapted to her circumstances, and be varied with different occasions. Thus, at breakfast, she should be attired in a very neat and simple manner, wearing no ornaments. If this dress should decidedly pertain only to the breakfast hour, and be specially suited for such domestic occupations as usually follow the meal, then it would be well to exchange it before the time of receiving visitors, if the mistress be in the habit of doing so. It is still to be remembered, however, that in changing the dress, jewellery and ornaments are not to be worn until the full dress for dinner is assumed.

———————

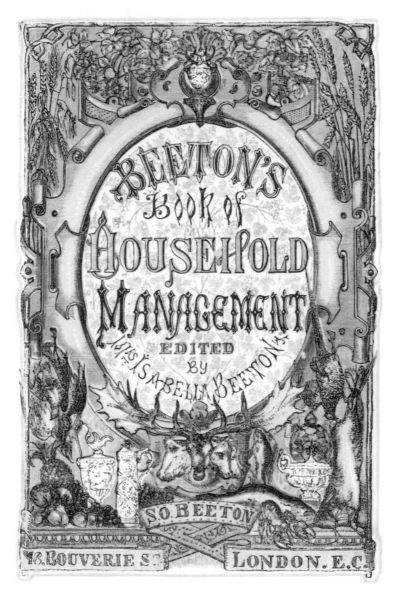

The first edition of Household Management.

'How kind the Lord has been to me' – a Victorian woman's acceptance of her lot, enshrined in tapestry work.

Copper pans in gleaming order. The Victorians were firm believers in a utensil for every occasion.

The well-scrubbed Victorian kitchen with all its paraphernalia. The drum in the foreground was used for cleaning knives.

A standard kitchen range with ovens below and warming cupboards above. Ashes were cleaned from the grate in the centre. This model was popular in many homes when Mrs Beeton wrote Household Management.

A working kitchen – hot water was a comparative novelty – hence the burnished copper pipes displayed with pride.

THE GIRLS OWN PAPER.   VOGELSANG & KAISER CHROMO - LITH. MUNICH.   LONDON.

PASTRY.   SANDWICHES.   FRUIT JELLY.   SALAD EGGS A LA RUSSE.   NOUGATS. SANDWICHES.   SWEETMEATS.   GALANTINE OF VEAL.
OYSTER PATTIES. BASKET OF FLOWERS. SANDWICHES.   FRUIT.   EPERGNE.   FRUIT. TRIFLE. BASKET OF FLOWERS. SANDWICHES.
FANCY CAKES.   GATEAU NAPOLITAIN.   MOCHA JELLY. SALAD EGGS A LA RUSSE. APRICOT CREAM. FANCY PASTRY.

HOW WE ENTERTAIN OUR FRIENDS – THE SUPPER TABLE

Advice on place-settings and table decoration was given in great detail in Household Management.

While a dress for every occasion was clearly *de rigeur* in a lady's wardrobe, she was also expected to take interest in the less fortunate beyond her gates. This was done by many with an oppressive sense of duty rather than with natural compassion, but there were many wealthy women who genuinely felt for the poor and worked hard to alleviate the effects of poverty around them. Mrs Beeton herself had strong views on the subject:

> Charity and benevolence are duties which a mistress owes to herself as well as to her fellow-creatures; and there is scarcely any income so small but something may be spared from it, even if it be but 'the widow's mite'. It is to be always remembered, however, that it is the *spirit* of charity which imparts to the gift a value far beyond its actual amount, and is by far its better part. Visiting the houses of the poor is the only practical way really to understand the actual state of each family; and although there may be difficulties in following out this plan in the metropolis and other large cities, yet in country towns and rural districts these objections do not obtain. Great advantages may result from visits paid to the poor; for there being unfortunately much ignorance generally amongst them with respect to all household knowledge, there will be opportunities for advising and instructing them in a pleasant and unobtrusive manner in cleanliness, industry, cookery and good management.

When the master caught a cold on a day's fishing, the staff could usually be relied upon to come up with a suitable home-made remedy.

Despite her own busy writing day, Isabella took time to practise what she preached. Even in the green fields of Pinner there was poverty and destitution, and she helped wherever she could. The winter of 1859 was very severe, and Pinner, along with most of the country, lay under deep snow. Frost lay on the ground for weeks, and at the end of December there was one of the worst blizzards on record.

Each week Isabella made eight or nine gallons of soup in her copper boiler to serve a dozen needy families in the village. 'The poor children of the neighbourhood came regularly with their cans for soup,' her sister Lucy recalled many years later. 'And each week they brought bigger cans.' The meat and vegetable soup, probably made from kitchen leftovers, was clearly delicious and a tribute to Mrs Beeton's emerging talents. The great Reform Club chef Alexis Soyer, whom Isabella admired, had already proved that one of the arts of cookery is economy and an ability to make the most of anything at hand.

Her soup supplemented the cottagers' meagre winter diet of cold meat and stale bread. It took six and a half hours to cook, and cost about a penny-ha'penny a quart. 'With a little more knowledge of the cooking art,' Mrs Beeton observed, 'they might have, for less expense, a warm dish every day.' Curiously for one who was such a stickler for detail, she refers to the year she made the soup as 1858, which was in fact an extremely mild winter when late autumn temperatures of 97 degrees Fahrenheit were recorded at Chiswick. The following year brought the weather which was to be remembered for generations. Isabella included the recipe for the soup in *Household Management*:

USEFUL SOUP FOR BENEVOLENT PURPOSES

INGREDIENTS: An ox-cheek, any pieces of trimmings of beef which may be bought very cheaply (say 4 lb), a few bones, any pot-liquor the larder may furnish, a quarter of a peck of onions, 6 leeks, a large bunch of herbs, half a pound of celery (the outside pieces, or green tops, do very well), half a pound of carrots, half a pound of turnips, half a pound of coarse brown sugar, half a pint of beer, 4 lb of common rice, or pearl barley, half a pound of salt, 1 oz of black pepper, a few raspings, 10 gallons of water.
MODE: Cut up the meat in small pieces, break the bones, put them in a copper with 10 gallons of water and stew for half an hour. Cut up the vegetables, put them in with the sugar and beer, and boil for 4 hours. Two hours before the soup is wanted, add the rice and raspings, and keep stirring till it is well mixed in the soup, which simmer gently. If the liquor reduces too much, fill up with water.
TIME: Six and a half hours. AVERAGE COST: Three-ha'pence per quart.

Mrs Beeton's ideal mistress led a very full day before her husband returned from the office in the evening. A typical daily routine, followed by thousands of Victorian women, is outlined for guidance. Had Isabella herself followed it to the letter, it is hardly likely that *Household Management* would have been written at all:

Having risen early, and having given due attention to the bath and made a careful toilet, it will be well at once to see that the children have received their proper ablutions, and are in every way clean and comfortable. The first meal of the day, breakfast, will then be served, at which all the family should be punctually present, unless illness or other circumstances prevent.

After breakfast is over it will be well for the mistress to make a round of the kitchen and other offices to see that all are in order, and that the morning's work has been properly performed by the various domestics. The orders for the day should then be given, and any questions which the domestics desire to ask, respecting their several departments, should be answered and any special articles they require handed to them from the store closet. In those establishments where there is a housekeeper, it will not be so necessary for the mistress personally to perform the above-named duties.

After this general superintendence of her servants the mistress, if the mother of a young family, may devote herself to the instruction of some of its younger members, or to the examination of the state of their wardrobe, leaving the later portion of the morning for reading, or for some amusing recreation. 'Recreation,' says Bishop Hall, 'is intended to the mind as whetting is to the scythe, to sharpen the edge of it which would otherwise grow dull and blunt.' Unless the means of the mistress be very circumscribed, and she be obliged to devote a great deal of her time to the making of children's clothes and other economical pursuits, it is right that she should give some time to the pleasures of literature, the innocent delights of the garden, and to the improvement of any special abilities for music, painting and other elegant arts which she may happily possess.

These duties and pleasures being performed and enjoyed, the hour of luncheon will have arrived. This is the very necessary meal between an early breakfast and a late dinner, as a healthy person with good exercise should have a fresh supply of food once in four hours. It should be a light meal, but its solidity must, of course, be in some degree proportionate to the time it is intended to enable you to wait for your dinner, and the amount of exercise you take in the meantime. At this time also, the servants' dinner will be served.

In many houses where a nursery dinner is provided for the children at about one o'clock, the mistress and the elder portion of the family make their luncheon at the same time from the same joint, or whatever may be provided. A mistress will arrange, according to circumstances, the serving of the meal; but the more usual plan is for the lady of the house to have the joint brought to her table, and afterwards carried to the nursery.

After luncheon morning calls and visits may be made and received. These may be divided under three heads: those of ceremony, friendship and congratulation or condolence. Visits of ceremony, or courtesy which occasionally merge into those of friendship are to be paid under various circumstances. Thus they are uniformly required after dining at a friend's house, or after a ball, picnic or any other party. These visits should be short, a stay from fifteen to twenty minutes being quite sufficient. A lady paying a visit may remove her boa or neckerchief, but neither her shawl nor bonnet.

When other visitors are announced it is as well to retire as soon as possible, taking care to let it appear that their arrival is not the cause. When they are quietly seated, and the bustle of their entrance is over, rise from your chair, taking a kind leave of the hostess and bowing politely to the guests.

Should you call at an inconvenient time, not having ascertained the luncheon hour, retire as soon as possible without, however, showing that you feel yourself an intruder. It is not difficult for any well-bred or even good-tempered person to know what to say on such an occason and, on politely withdrawing, a promise can be made to call again, if the lady you have called upon appears really disappointed.

It was, of course, essential to look one's best. When in doubt about what to wear a lady could always consult her personal maid – as a species they had a reputation for pouring over fashion magazines in their spare time. Many possibly had a more instinctive idea of style than their mistresses or, at the very least, were keen to make suggestions. In fact, Mrs Beeton positively encouraged it:

A waiting maid who wishes to make herself useful will study the fashion books with attention, so as to be able to aid her mistress's judgement in dressing according to the prevailing fashion, with such modification as her style of countenance requires . . . The exigencies of fashion and luxury are such that all ladies, except those of the very highest rank, will consider themselves fortunate in having about them a thoughtful person, capable of diverting their finery to a useful purpose.

An observant lady's maid could always advise on the latest fashions. Some, however, could be a little too observant.

The mistress found her personal maid indispensable in helping her to face the world.

1878.

TRIUMPH OF ART.

"AND NOW MA'AM, I HOPE THAT'LL PLAZE YE; SHURE THERE'S NIVER A SOUL AS WOULD THINK IT WAS YOUR OWN HAIR!"

The duties of the lady's-maid revolved mainly around keeping her mistress's clothes and shoes clean and in a good state of repair, hairdressing, helping her to dress and arranging the dressing table. Many were sent for hairdressing lessons, and the best could always be relied on to have their own recipes for hair preparations and beauty care. One of her tasks was to dress her mistress before breakfast, ready to face the day and, in giving some useful tips, Mrs Beeton must have suppressed a wry smile when she warned: 'In arranging the petticoat, a careful lady's-maid will see that it is firmly fastened around the waist.' The effects of any slackness would obviously have been unthinkable!

In the small and convenient homes of today it is difficult to imagine what an enormous task it was to run a house in Mrs Beeton's time. Often there were so many staff that the problem of feeding them meant, in effect, budgeting for two large families. A conscientious mistress would take on responsibility for her employees' welfare, as well as what amounted to the work of a wages clerk:

The following table of average yearly wages paid to domestics, with the various members of the household placed in the order in which they are usually ranked, will serve as a guide to regulate the expenditure of an establishment:

	When not found in Livery.	When found in Livery.
The House Steward	From £40 to £80	—
The Valet	„ 25 to 50	From £20 to £30
The Butler	„ 25 to 50	—
The Cook	„ 20 to 40	—
The Gardener	„ 20 to 40	—
The Footman	„ 20 to 40	„ 15 to 25
The Under Butler	„ 15 to 30	„ 15 to 25
The Coachman	—	„ 20 to 35
The Groom	„ 15 to 30	„ 12 to 20
The Under Footman	—	„ 12 to 20
The Page or Footboy	„ 8 to 18	„ 6 to 14
The Stableboy	„ 6 to 12	—

	When no extra allowance is made for Tea, Sugar, and Beer.	When an extra allowance is made for Tea, Sugar, and Beer.
The Housekeeper	From £20 to £45	From £18 to £40
The Lady's-maid	„ 12 to 25	„ 10 to 20
The Head Nurse	„ 15 to 30	„ 13 to 26
The Cook	„ 14 to 30	„ 12 to 26
The Upper Housemaid	„ 12 to 20	„ 10 to 17
The Upper Laundry-maid	„ 12 to 18	„ 10 to 15
The Maid-of-all-work	„ 9 to 14	„ 7½ to 11
The Under Housemaid	„ 8 to 12	„ 6½ to 10
The Still-room Maid	„ 9 to 14	„ 8 to 13
The Nursemaid	„ 8 to 12	„ 5 to 10
The Under Laundry-maid	„ 9 to 14	„ 8 to 12
The Kitchen-maid	„ 9 to 14	„ 8 to 12
The Scullery-maid	„ 5 to 9	„ 4 to 8

These quotations of wages are those usually given in or near the metropolis; but, of course, there are many circumstances connected with locality, and also having reference to the long service on the one hand, or the inexperience on the other, of domestics, which may render the wages still higher or lower than those named above. All the domestics mentioned in the above table would enter into the establishment of a wealthy nobleman. The number of servants, of course, would become smaller in proportion to the lesser size of the establishment; and we may here enumerate a scale of servants suited to various incomes, commencing with—

About £1,000 a year—A cook, upper housemaid, nursemaid, under housemaid, and a man servant.

About £750 a year—A cook, housemaid, nursemaid, and footboy.

About £500 a year—A cook, housemaid, and nursemaid.

About £300 a year—A maid-of-all-work and nursemaid.

About £200 or £150 a year—A maid-of-all-work (and girl occasionally).

Housemaids were expected to be discreet – but could they always be trusted?

COMMANDERS IN CRINOLINES

Homes both great and small sailed majestically through the seasons like the flagships of the middle classes. Upstairs the saloons sparkled spotlessly, while down below the engine-room was a constant bustle of controlled activity.

Mrs Beeton gives an intriguing insight into the servants' year:

The spring is the usual period set apart for house-cleaning and removing all the dust and dirt which will necessarily, with the best of housewives, accumulate during the winter months from the smoke of the coal, oil and gas. The season is also well adapted for washing and bleaching linen as the weather, not being then too hot for the exertions necessary in washing counterpanes, blankets and heavy things in general, the work is better and more easily done than in the intense heats of July, which month some recommend for these purposes. Winter curtains should be taken down and replaced by the summer white ones; and furs and woollen cloths also carefully laid by. The former should be well shaken and brushed, and then pinned upon paper or linen, with camphor to preserve them from the moths. Furs will be preserved in the same way.

Included under the general description of house-cleaning must be understood, turning out all the nooks and corners of drawers, cupboards, lumber-rooms and lofts, with a view to getting rid of all unnecessary articles, which only create dirt and attract vermin; sweeping of chimneys, taking up carpets, painting and whitewashing the kitchen and offices, papering rooms when needed and, generally speaking, the house putting on with the approaching summer a bright appearance and a new face, in unison with nature. Oranges should now be preserved and orange wine made.

The summer will be found, in consequence of the diminuation of labour for domestics, the best period for examining and repairing household linen, and for 'putting to rights' all those articles which have received a large share of wear and tear during the dark winter days. In direct reference to this matter we may here remark that sheets should be turned 'sides to middle' before they are allowed to get very thin. Otherwise patching, which is uneconomical from the time it consumes, and is unsightly in point of appearance, will have to be resorted to.

Hard-worked, and with little to smile about, the staff of a large house pose for a photograph.

In June and July gooseberries, currants, raspberries, strawberries and other summer fruits should be preserved, and jams and jellies made. In July, too, the making of walnut ketchup should be attended to, as the green walnuts will be approaching perfection for this purpose. Mixed pickles may also now be made, and it will be found a good plan to have ready a jar of pickle-juice into which to put occasionally some young french beans or cauliflowers.

In the early autumn plums of various kinds are to be bottled and preserved and jams and jellies made. A little later, tomato sauce, a most useful article to have by you, may be prepared; a supply of apples laid in, if you have a place to keep them, as also a few keeping pears and filberts. Endeavour to keep also a large vegetable marrow – it will be found delicious in the winer.

In October and November it will be necessary to prepare for the cold weather, and get ready the winter clothing for the various members of the family. The white summer curtains will now be carefully put away, the fireplaces, grates and chimneys looked to, and the house put in a thorough state of repair, so that no 'loose tile' may, at a future day, interfere with your comfort, and extract something considerable from your pocket.

In December, the principal duty lies in preparing for the creature comforts of those near and dear to us, so as to meet old Christmas with a happy face, a contented mind and a full larder; and in stoning the plums, washing the currants, cutting the citron, beating the eggs and mixing the pudding, a housewife is not unworthily greeting the genial season of all good things.

Up on the bridge, the mistress prepared to guide the fortunes of the house through another year, and keep its affairs on an even course. In Isabella's eyes it was one of the finest achievements a woman could aspire to, and she was unstinting in praise and encouragement for her 'sisters':

She ought to remember that she is the first and last, the Alpha and Omega in the government of her establishment; and that it is by her conduct that its whole internal policy is regulated. She is therefore a person of far more importance in a community than she usually thinks she is. On her pattern her daughters model themselves; by her counsels they are directed; through her virtues all are honoured . . .

The world was sad! the garden was a wild!
And man the hermit sigh'd till *woman* smiled.

. . . Let the mistress of every house rise to the responsibility of its management; so that, in doing her duty to all around her, she may receive the genuine reward of respect, love and affection!

4
The Art of Dining
Mrs Beeton on Food

If Mrs Beeton had not been quite so strong-willed and singleminded, generations of women would possibly never have benefited from the wisdom of *Household Management*. Before plunging seriously into cookery writing she sought the advice of a Mrs English, a friend of her parents who was regarded as something of a cookery expert. Mrs English, a forceful woman, took the Victorian view that writing of any kind was no business for a woman. But sensing Isabella's enthusiasm, she wrote:

I see difficulties in your way as regards publishing a book on cookery. Cookery is a science that is only learnt by long experience and years of study, which of course you have not had. Therefore my advice would be to compile a book of receipts from a variety of the best books published on cookery, and Heaven knows there is a great variety for you to choose from.

It was hardly encouraging, but Isabella was not easily dissuaded. *Household Management* was Sam's idea, aimed at attracting both the readers of his *Englishwoman's Domestic Magazine* and *Beeton's Dictionary of Universal Information*. It was Isabella's skill and dedication over the next four years which turned it into a classic of its kind.

Sam appealed to readers of the *Englishwoman's Domestic Magazine* to send in recipes for publication, and the trickle soon turned into a torrent of more than 2000. He had always encouraged reader participation, partly because it was a reliable indicator of which articles were popular, but also because he passionately believed that women should play a more active part in the world around them. Mrs Beeton, with common sense and eye for economy, sifted them carefully for likely entries.

While some recipes had to be adapted to suit the book, others were discarded as unsuitable or impractical. A message to 'A.B.C. of Bolton' appeared in one issue of the magazine: 'You do not mention whether the recipes have been tested by you. We should have preferred if you had borne testimony to their worth.' When the list was pared down, Isabella relied on standard recipes from other books – particularly Eliza Acton's *Modern Cookery For Private Families*, a slightly down-market but nevertheless superb cookbook published in 1845. By the time *Household Management* appeared Eliza Acton, mercifully for the Beeton's, had passed away.

Sam, meanwhile, was appealing for more: 'We shall be exceedingly obliged to any lady who will spare a few moments to write out for us some of her choicest recipes, and thus make the *Englishwoman's Domestic Magazine* a means whereby her knowledge and skill may be communicated to the world for the benefit of all.' Isabella also begged recipes from friends and acquaintences – among them Baroness Pudding from the Baroness de Tessier in Epsom; Soup à la Solferino from a foreign correspondent who was at the battle; and Soup à la Cantatrice from singer Jenny Lind, who believed that it was good for the voice. Of the final selection of 1500 or so, possibly only one was contributed by Isabella herself, the Soup for Benevolent Purposes which she had served to the poor of Pinner.

Isabella, on the other hand, never claimed that the recipes were her own. She describes herself throughout the book as 'the editress', and thanks readers profusely for their contributions. 'A large private circle has also rendered me considerable service,' she adds. 'A diligent study of the best modern writers on cookery was also necessary to the faithful fulfillment of my task.

It is ironic that half a century later, when large families were less popular, the number of domestic servants was dwindling and some items of food were not as plentiful, that Mrs Beeton became a music hall byword for extravagance. Sayings attributed to her, such as 'first catch your hare', and 'take six dozen eggs' were, in fact, never used by her in the book. She did, as we shall see, indulge in recipes which may seem over the top by our standards, but not when we consider that some Victorians really did stage picnics for forty people and ball-suppers for eighty.

Humorist Wyndham Lewis was among those still milking the misconception in 1924, with a witty playlet in the *Daily Mail*:

THE ART OF DINING

MRS BEETON: This is a simple little sauce composed expressly for persons with limited incomes, and may be recommended to any housewife with frugal tastes and, indeed, to the poorest.

LORD HYBROUGH: Perhaps Mrs Beeton will reveal the secret? We – (*He sweeps the whole room with a wide gesture*) – we are all comrades here.

MRS BEETON (*coyly*): It is a very poor, unpretentious little thing. (*Closing her eyes*) Take half a gallon of Napoleon brandy, place in a silver pan, rinse round and throw away. Next take five pounds of cream and break into it the yolks of thirty eggs. Whisk over a slow fire and set on ice. Next take a quart of Imperial Tokay, three pounds of fine sugar, and ten lemons. Mix thoroughly, strain through the cream mixture and throw away. Take a dozen more eggs, beat lightly into a froth with two quarts of good Madeira, squeeze in the juice of a pound of hothouse grapes, and pour over the residue. After standing for an hour strain the whole through a fine sieve and throw away as before. Repeat from the beginning adding a magnum of champagne, the whites of two dozen plovers' eggs . . .

Wyndham Lewis loved stand-up targets, but it was easy to forget that, in the days after the First World War, many of the plain ingredients Mrs Beeton used, such as butter, eggs, milk, cheese and vegetables were cheap in her day. Only meat had risen substantially in price. The mistress of a typical middle-class house could find herself budgeting for up to fifteen people, if one includes the servants. Mrs Beeton's aim was not, as many later believed, to introduce gourmet cooking to a select few, but to preach nutrition and economy to a broad stream of society.

It was only in 1932, when the National Portrait Gallery exhibited her now-famous photograph, that *Household Management* began to again receive wide attention and a long-overdue reappraisal. Thousands of Victorian readers who had followed her ground-rules almost religiously were long dead, and a new generation was to discover the book's delights.

HOG NOT BACON

Lord Bacon was about to pass sentence of death on a man of the name of Hogg, when the prisoner said with an expression of arch confidence: 'I claim indulgence, my lord, on the plea of relationship; for I am convinced your lordship will never be unnatural enough to hang one of your own family.'

'Indeed,' replied the judge with some amazement. 'I was not aware that I had the honour of your alliance. Perhaps you will be good enough to name the degree of our mutual affinity.'

'My name, my lord, is Hogg,' replied the impudent thief. 'Your lordship's is Bacon, and all then will allow that bacon and hog are very closely allied.'

'I am sorry,' replied his lordship. 'I cannot allow the truth of your insistance. Hog cannot be bacon until it is hanged. So before I can admit your plea, or acknowledge the family compact, Hogg must be hanged tomorrow morning.'

Household Management

Her preface to the book sums up her intentions perhaps better than all the reviews and criticism put together:

I must frankly own that, had I known beforehand the labour which this book has entailed, I should never have been courageous enough to commence it. What moved me in the first instance to attempt a work like this was the discomfort and suffering which I had seen brought about by household mismanagement. I have always thought that there is no more fruitful source of family discontent than badly cooked dinners and untidy ways.

The *New Statesman*, reassessing her masterpiece in 1932, concluded:

There is none of the amoral nonsense of modern times which offers us delicious banquets with an air of 'eat, drink and be merry, for tomorrow we die'. There is no taint of the Epicurean gourmet in Mrs Beeton's phrasing. Her purpose is not to lure us into a paradise of dishes, but to allay discomfort and suffering, and to make an end of family discontent.

If she believed in the principle 'feed the brute', she did so in order to convert him into something better. Without the help of any of Pavlov's experiments, she realized that the male monster could be taught to associate happiness with a perfect under-done steak, and that little children looking on a well-cooked, well-carved goose would be in a mood to lead better lives.

Even the *Daily Mirror*, the voice of the common people, was unstinting in its praise of the National Portrait Gallery picture:

All good housewives and grateful husbands will doubtless go and look at the lady who has done so much for them in a womanly way.

We have been told that cooking in England is a lost art. We are a nation of gluttons rather than gourmets. We eat, we do not dine.

If this is true, it is not Mrs Beeton's fault. In her short life she produced the classic guide to the preparation of food. Any menu of hers is enough to give us a healthy appreciation of the pleasures of the table.

We are glad that Mrs Beeton has come to rest among our immortals. There will be other feminists in the National Portrait Gallery, the suffragette, the actress and the long-distance flier.

We take off our hat to them all, but especially to Mrs Beeton, who brought such a magical touch to cooking that her book is a perpetual joy.

To discover why *Household Management* merited such praise a century after publication, and still does, it is important to see it against the eating habits of the time. One critic said that Mrs Beeton lived in an age when Englishmen were going all over the world 'teaching the heathen in his blindness how not to cook a cabbage, how not to make rice pudding and how not to make coffee.' It is true that the vast majority of people had almost no notion of basic nutrition. It had taken a Frenchman, Alexis Soyer, to teach simple cooking to English soldiers in the Crimea. Before he arrived they had been boiling meat in their socks and throwing the meat stock away. Soyer believed in peasant principles of waste-not-want-not, and made use of every available scrap of food. Mrs Beeton herself could not help remarking, when doling out her Soup for Benevolent Purposes, that with a little rudimentary knowledge the poor would have survived with fewer problems.

Despite plentiful produce in the shops, food was adulterated with probably even more additives than today. Our idea of good old-fashioned wholesome food was largely a myth. While we struggle to come to terms with preservative E223, anti-oxident E301 and colour red 2G, the Victorians had their own problems. Since it first arrived in Britain, tea had been mixed with anything from potato leaves to deadly nightshade; cocoa eked out with brick-dust had been common since Regency days. Unscrupulous traders watered milk and restored the colour with powdered chalk; flour was whitened with plaster of Paris. Butchers often left all the blood in carcasses to increase their weight, while bakers secretly added crushed bones to their bread mixtures.

The situation became so out of hand that the *Lancet* led a campaign against shopkeepers and manufacturers who adulterated sugar with white lead and put alum with bread by publishing their names and addresses. After years of *exposés* and pressure, the *Lancet* finally achieved the passing of the 1860 Adulteration Act which saw the appointment of county analysts. Mrs Beeton stressed that food should only be bought from reputable dealers, and preferably delivered to the house, where it could be offered for inspection.

Provision merchants were well-patronized, though Mrs Beeton preferred tradesmen to call and offer their goods for inspection at the door.

FRENCH BEEF

It has been all but universally admitted that the beef of France is
greatly inferior in quality to that of England, owing to the inferiority
of pasturage. M. Curmer, however, one of the latest writers on the
culinary art, tells us that this is a vulgar error, and that French beef
is far superior to that of England . . .

A Frenchman was one day blandly remonstrating against the
supercilious scorn expressed by Englishmen for the beef of France.
'I have been two times in England,' he remarked, 'but I nevere find
the bif so superieur to ours. I find it vary conveenient that they bring
it you on leetle pieces of stick, for one penny – but I do not find the
bif superieur.' On hearing this the Englishman, red with
astonishment, exclaimed: 'Good heavens, sir! You have been eating
cat's meat.'

No M. Curmer, we are ready to acknowledge the superiority of
your cookery, but we have long since made up our minds as to the
inferiority of your raw material.

Household Management

Household Management was never intended to be a mere recipe book. Mrs
Beeton set out to educate women in domestic science, and constantly drove
home the message of hygiene and nutrition. Most of Britain's eight million
working men and women had acquired the habit of taking bread and cheese for
the short meal-breaks at work, and having a hot dinner when they returned in
the evening. In many cases it was cooked with complete ignorance of the need
for a balanced diet. The rocketing price of meat meant that the poor could
afford only bacon.

The lower-middle classes had better food but, like everyone else, were
unable to preserve it for more than a few days at a time. Mrs Beeton offered
a variety of curries, hashes and cold joints, though higher up the scale using the
left-overs was considered socially inferior. Some middle- and upper-class
families preferred to throw the remains of each meal away rather than give the
impression that they were recycling it.

The middle classes were the fastest-growing social group – the 1851 Census
recorded 272,000 professional workers, and within two decades the figure had
tripled. Most of them ate during the day in dining houses and restaurants which
were springing up in their thousands, and often lingered for an evening meal

before returning home. Sam Beeton, like many of this new, ambitious social group, was often late home from the office. While Isabella and Sam lived as equals, she preached to her fellow women that the best place for a man to receive nourishment was at home under the supervision of his wife.

This was one of her prime reasons for writing the book. In the original preface she warns her 'sisters': 'Men are now so well-served out of doors – at their clubs, well-ordered taverns and dining houses that, in order to compete with the attractions of these places, a mistress must be thoroughly acquainted with the theory and practice of cookery, as well as be perfectly conversant with all the other arts of making and keeping a beautiful home.' From the beginning it was clear that Mrs Beeton intended her book to be rather more than a cookery book. Its real significance lies in the way she placed cookery in the social scheme of things, and gave it an importance that no one previously had fully realized. An academic, writing much later at the time of women's suffrage, claimed that 'Mrs Beetonism has preserved the family as a social unit, and made social reform a possibility' and, who knows, he may even have been right.

SADDLE OF BEEF

Brillat Savarin tells the story of a Croat captain whom he invited to dinner in 1815, during the occupation of Paris by the allied troops. This officer was amazed at his host's preparations, and said: 'When we are campaigning and get hungry, we knock over the first animal we can find, cut off a steak, powder it with salt, put it under the saddle, gallop over it for half a mile, and then dine like princes.'

Household Management

While Mrs Beeton saw problems in the eating habits of the masses, her own class had its peculiarities too. Food among the wealthy had become a status symbol – not in the costliness of dishes, but in their variety. Anyone who could provide a dinner table groaning under a gargantuan spread was considered a social force to be reckoned with. Mrs Beeton reflected the trend by cramming her book with an enormous number of recipes, covering every permutation of popular food. It was partly from thoroughness and her natural instinct for selling books, but she tempered the breathtaking list with nuggets of domestic science which made women more conscious of their role in the home.

I have striven to make my work something more than a cookery book, and have therefore, on the best authority that I could obtain, given an account of the natural history of the animals and vegetables which we use as food. I have followed the animal from his birth to his appearance on the table; have described the manner of feeding him, and of slaying him, the position of his various joints and, after giving the recipes, have described the modes of carving meat, poultry and game.

She gave, too, detailed information on the changes food undergoes when cooked. No one previously had written with such extraordinary authority on, say, the roasting of meat:

When meat is properly roasted, the outer layer of its albumen is coagulated, and thus presents a barrier to the exit of the juice. In roasting meat, the heat must be strongest at first, and it should then be much reduced. To have a good juicy roast, therefore, the fire must be red and vigorous at the very commencement of the operation. In the most careful roasting, some of the juice is squeezed out of the meat: this evaporates on the surface of the meat and gives it a dark brown colour, a rich lustre, and a strong aromatic taste. Besides these effects on the albumen and the expelled juice, roasting converts the cellular tissue of the meat into gelatine, and melts the fat out of the fat cells.

Mrs Beeton also had a working knowledge of the digestive system, and gave advice on how various meats should be cooked:

White meats, and the meat of young animals, require to be very well roasted, both to be pleasant to the palate and easy of digestion. Thus, veal, pork and lamb should be thoroughly done to the centre. Mutton and beef, on the other hand, do not generally speaking require to be so thoroughly done, and they should be dressed to the point that, in carving them, the gravy should just run, but not too freely.

In the days before widespread anxiety about cholesterol she had little taste for fatty food, and appears to be a pioneer of the kitchen roll: 'All dishes fried in fat should be placed before the fire on a piece of blotting paper, or sieve reversed, and left there for a few minutes, so that any superfluous greasy moisture may be removed.'

The whole business of frying, like all methods of cooking, was explained in minute detail, so that women would know exactly what processes were taking place. She acquired a phenomenal amount of technical information in a comparatively short time by reading around the subject, talking to experts and consulting Sam's all-embracing *Dictionary of Universal Information*:

The philosophy of frying consists in this, that liquids subjected to the action of fire do not all receive the same quantity of heat. Being differently constituted in their nature, they possess different 'capacities for caloric'. Thus, you may with impunity dip your finger in boiling spirits of wine; you should take it very quickly from boiling brandy, yet more rapidly from water.

As a consequence of this, heated fluids act differently on the sapid bodies presented to them. Those put in water dissolve, and are reduced to a soft mass, the result being bouillon, stock etc. Those or less deep colour and are finally carbonized. The reason for these different results is that, in the first instance, water dissolves and extracts the interior juices of the alimentary substances placed in it; whilst, in the second, the juices are preserved, for they are insoluble in oil.

There is little doubt that, to write with such authority, the kitchen at Chandos Villas would have closely resembled the laboratory Mrs Beeton likened it to. Her cook must have been both patient and quite well-paid to assist in the hectic daily experiments conducted on Isabella's well-scrubbed table. Isabella's sister Lucy stayed at Pinner as a young girl, and later recalled: 'No recipe went into the book without a successful trial, and the house was the scene of many experiments and some failures. I remember Isabella coming out of the kitchen one day. "This won't do at all," she said, and gave me the cake that had turned out like a biscuit. I thought it was very good. It had currents in it.'

Mrs Beeton was prepared to test as much as time would allow and, while the recipes may not have been hers, they are written with a distinct air of first-hand experience. Her recipe for 'An Excellent Pickle', however, carries the conscientious footnote: 'This recipe was forwarded by a subscriber to the *Englishwoman's Domestic Magazine*. Mrs Beeton, not having tested it, cannot vouch for its excellence but the contributor spoke very highly in its favour.' One can almost see her laying out the utensils like surgical instruments, followed by the ingredients in order of use. Her cooking methods, and a keen awareness of whom she was writing for, led her to become possibly the first cookery editor to lay out recipes – listing ingredients, cooking time and cost – in a way which has been copied ever since.

Mrs Beeton's suggestions for meals are sprinkled with humour, anecdotes, poetry and her own sayings, such as 'a place for everything and everything in its place', and 'clean as you go for muddle makes more muddle'. She was fond of classical references, too, quoting Pliny, Linnaeus and Homer as she led her housewives on a pilgrim's progress of the kitchen. In telling them how to make parsley butter, for instance, she digresses to point out that soldiers fed their chariot horses on parsley in Homer's *Iliad*; how Pliny saw it as a sign of mourning; and the story of its first journey to Europe, from Egypt, via Sardinia to Marseilles. A cross-reference then takes them into tales of parsley in ancient Greece, and how 'the voluptuous Anacreon' sang its praises.

From time to time *Household Management* soars above mere domesticity into literary delights which take the reader by surprise. Her 'General Observations on the Common Hog' contain an unforgettable description of the runt of the litter:

> A poor, little shrivelled half-starved anatomy with a small, melancholy voice, a staggering gait, a woe-begon countenance and a thread of a tail, whose existence the complacent mother ignores, his plethoric brothers and sisters repudiate, and for whose emaciated jaws there is never a spare supplemental teat till one of the favoured gormandizers, overtaken by momentary oblivion, drops the lacteal fountain and gives the little squeaking struggler the chance of a momentary mouthful.

For reasons which no one has successfully fathomed, Mrs Beeton positively blooms on the subject of pigs. She clearly has a weakness for them – a 'grandiose pathos', as someone once commented. She even wanders off into the interesting question of the status of pigs in the Bible. If they were considered so universally unclean, and unfit for human consumption, she asks, then why does the Bible contain so many references to herds of swine? As they trot through the Old and New Testament in droves – why were they kept at all? Mrs Beeton's keen, inquiring mind strayed into many such byways, and her journalistic idiosyncracies make *Household Management* a joy to read. But pigs especially fascinated her – at times she is almost sentimental about them – and, unlike any of the other animals she describes in great detail, the suggestion of cruelty to pigs makes her flare with indignation. She lambasts owners who put rings through their pigs' noses with such passion that one fears for any hapless breeder who might have crossed her path.

Despite her fondness, the pig, like most creatures great and small, was considered well worthy of the Victorian table. One of her recipes, for ten people, requires a whole sucking pig, presenting a formidable task to the carver. Even Mrs Beeton admits: 'It seems at first sight rather an elaborate dish to carve, but by carefully mastering the details of the business, every difficulty will vanish. If a partial failure be at first made, all embarrassment will quickly disappear on a second trial.' By which time, hopefully, the guests would not have been driven elsewhere by sheer hunger.

Household Management is largely a manual of plain cooking in which basic food, perfectly prepared and presented, could be turned into the most

BILL OF FARE FOR A PICNIC FOR 40 PERSONS.

2149. A joint of cold roast beef, a joint of cold boiled beef, 2 ribs of lamb, 2 shoulders of lamb, 4 roast fowls, 2 roast ducks, 1 ham, 1 tongue, 2 veal-and-ham pies, 2 pigeon pies, 6 medium-sized lobsters, 1 piece of collared calf's head, 18 lettuces, 6 baskets of salad, 6 cucumbers.

2150. Stewed fruit well sweetened, and put into glass bottles well corked ; 3 or 4 dozen plain pastry biscuits to eat with the stewed fruit, 2 dozen fruit turnovers, 4 dozen cheesecakes, 2 cold cabinet puddings in moulds, 2 blanc-manges in moulds, a few jam puffs, 1 large cold plum-pudding (this must be good), a few baskets of fresh fruit, 3 dozen plain biscuits, a piece of cheese, 6 lbs. of butter (this, of course, includes the butter for tea), 4 quartern loaves of household bread, 3 dozen rolls, 6 loaves of tin bread (for tea), 2 plain plum cakes, 2 pound cakes, 2 sponge cakes, a tin of mixed biscuits, ½ lb. of tea. Coffee is not suitable for a picnic, being difficult to make.

Things not to be forgotten at a Picnic.

2151. A stick of horseradish, a bottle of mint-sauce well corked, a bottle of salad dressing, a bottle of vinegar, made mustard, pepper, salt, good oil, and-pounded sugar. If it can be managed, take a little ice. It is scarcely necessary to say that plates, tumblers, wine-glasses, knives, forks, and spoons, must not be forgotten ; as also teacups and saucers, 3 or 4 teapots, some lump sugar, and milk, if this last-named article cannot be obtained in the neighbourhood. Take 3 corkscrews.

2152. *Beverages.*—3 dozen quart bottles of ale, packed in hampers; ginger-beer, soda-water, and lemonade, of each 2 dozen bottles ; 6 bottles of sherry, 6 bottles of claret, champagne à discrétion, and any other light wine that may be preferred, and 2 bottles of brandy. Water can usually be obtained so it is useless to take it.

delightful and delicious dishes. But here and there loom enormous meals of
gothic proportions. When we consider, for instance, a modern picnic where
lightness (on both the car springs and the digestion) is considered essential, the
Victorian equivalent is staggering. A commando unit could live effortlessly for
several weeks on the food consumed in the course of an afternoon-out a
hundred and fifty years ago.

Surprisingly, Isabella had little taste herself for daunting spreads. Large
dinner parties were popular with the family at Epsom before she married, with
the usual formidable array of dishes the middle classes felt obliged to offer. She

2142.—BILL OF FARE FOR A BALL SUPPER FOR 60 PERSONS (for Winter).

Boar's Head, garnished with Aspic Jelly.

Lobster Salad. | Fruited Jelly. | Mayonnaise of Fowl. | Charlotte Russe. | Lobster Salad.

Small Pastry. Small Ham, garnished. Iced Savoy Cake. Biscuits.

Two Roast Fowls, cut up. | Vanilla Cream. | Epergne, with Fruit. | Fruited Jelly. | Two Roast Fowls, cut up.

Prawns. Biscuits. Two Boiled Fowls, with Béchamel Sauce. Tongue, ornamented. Prawns. Small Pastry.

Custards, in glasses. Trifle, ornamented. Custards, in glasses.

Raised Chicken Pie.

Lobster Salad. | Fruited Jelly. | Tipsy Cake. Roast Pheasant. | Swiss Cream. | Lobster Salad.

Meringues. Epergne, with Fruit. Meringues.

Two Roast Fowls, cut up. | Raspberry Cream. | Galantine of Veal. Tipsy Cake. Raised Game Pie. | Fruited Jelly. Biscuits. | Two Roast Fowls, cut up.

Small Pastry.

Custards, in glasses. Trifle, ornamented. Custards, in glasses.

Prawns. Biscuits. Tongue, ornamented. Two Boiled Fowls, with Béchamel Sauce. Prawns. Small Pastry.

EPERGNE, WITH FRUIT.

Lobster Salad. | Fruited Jelly. Charlotte Russe. | Iced Savoy Cake. Small Ham, garnished. Mayonnaise of Fowl. Larded Capon. | Blancmange. Fruited Jelly. | Lobster Salad.

65

confessed that she found them 'a terrible ordeal', and once confided that 'a good dance somewhere is much more my line.' Nevertheless, Mrs Beeton gave her readers what they expected. Some table-plans were so elaborate that she was forced at one point to add: 'The length of the page will not admit of our giving the dishes as they should be placed on the table.'

The overwhelming choice of dishes was an extension of the Victorian's love of clutter. Homes of the wealthy middle classes may have sprouted in a frenzy of escapist architecture, but interior decor followed very narrow lines. Every wall was covered, every table, the piano and mantelpiece laden with bric-à-brac as though a passing swarm of sentimental trivia had flown in and settled on each surface. It reaffirmed the Victorians' belief in home and family and, in providing so much to occupy the attention, possibly helped them forget the

2143.—BILL OF FARE FOR A BALL SUPPER,

Or a Cold Collation for a Summer Entertainment, or Wedding or Christening Breakfast for 70 or 80 Persons (July).

world outside. In a world where men made the decisions while women flitted around the periphery, architecture and furniture were ponderous to the point of vulgarity, and knick-knacks delicate and twee. The obsessive overloading of gloomy rooms spread inevitably to the dining-table, which creaked under five-course dinners, often with a choice of up to ten desserts. Dining became an occasion which frequently took up most of the evening, and was elevated to an art – though Mrs Beeton was never a believer in art for art's sake. 'Dine we must,' she said, 'and we may as well dine elegantly as well as wholesomely.' After all she stressed to her readers, dining with dignity was the privilege of civilization:

The rank which a people occupy in the grand scale may be measured in their way of taking their meals, as well as by their way of treating their women. The nation which knows how to dine has learnt the leading lesson of progress. It implies both the will and the skill to reduce order, and surround with idealisms and graces, the more material conditions of human existence; and wherever that will and that skill exist, life cannot be wholly ignoble.

Such high sentiments did little to steady the nerves of a housewife planning a dinner party for her husband's friends, however aware she might be of her importance in the scheme of things. Isabella, remembering the nerve-wracking dinner marathons of her single years, was ever ready to leap to the rescue:

The half-hour before dinner is the great ordeal through which the mistress, in giving a dinner party, will either pass with flying colours, or lose many of her laurels. The anxiety to receive her guests – her hope that all will be present in due time – her trust in the skill of her cook and the attention of the other domestics, all tend to make the few minutes a trying time. The mistress, however, must display no kind of agitation, but show her tact in suggesting light and cheerful subjects of conversation which will be much aided by the introduction of any particularly new book, curiosity of art or article of virtue which may pleasantly engage the attention of the company. Photograph albums, crest albums, new music will aid to pass a few moments pleasantly.

Informed views on the latest books could be culled from the helpful pages of the *Englishwoman's Domestic Magazine*, along with ideas for 'artistic dinner cards'.

————————

These cards, about the size of a lady's ordinary card, are beautifully designed in colours, and contain charming groups of children engaged in various sports, pastimes and amusements, a white space being left for the inscription of a guest's name. These are infinitely prettier at the dinner table than the plain cards ordinarily used, and at once suggest topics for lively conversation, suggestions which to some will not be ungrateful or unwelcome.

————————

Silence was clearly not golden at such moments, and a trickle of polite, if thin, conversation presumably allayed any suspicion that their hostess may have been going through hell. From our viewpoint it seems not only another age but another world, yet Mrs Beeton's wisdom and down-to-earth advice helped many a Victorian woman achieve her ideal of a happy home.

As the *Evening News* aptly said at her centenary:

————————

Soldiers and statesmen may change the destinies of nations; but as promoters of human happiness they do not compare with cooks. . . . Mrs Beeton's grouse pies and her hierarchies of pliable domestics are today but an empty ritual of the mind. She remains, nevertheless, enshrined for ever in the British heart, the tutelary goddess of orderly living, the Confucius of the kitchen, the benefactress of a million homes, the illustrious patroness of good digestion waiting on appetite.

————————

5
The Beeton Track
In the Footsteps of an Extraordinary Victorian Couple

Seldom has a photograph aroused such curiosity as the rather severe studio portrait of Mrs Beeton which was unveiled at the National Portrait Gallery half a century ago. Thousands of visitors filed past the pensive study to see for the first time a woman whose name was as familiar as the family shopping list. The only clue to her private life was a few lines printed on the back of a postcard they queued to buy at the kiosk in the foyer:

Isabella Beeton

> To four generations of housewives Mrs Beeton's classic *Book of Household Management* has been a practical guide and daily companion. She married, in 1856, S. O. Beeton, an editor and publisher of exceptional ability; they were mutually helpful in their literary work, and to his inspiration her own book, distinguished by its intellectual and interesting qualities, owes it origin. The mother of four sons, she died aged 28, leaving the memory of a good, lovely and gifted woman.

In an age when men ran society so totally that few women even dared to yearn for individuality, Mrs Beeton emerged like a thorny rose from a bed of shrinking violets. Her independence, intellectual outlook and no-nonsense approach blossomed when she married Sam Beeton. It was lurking there all the time, waiting to be released; as a girl she was capable and caring, the kind of daughter the whole family leaned on in times of crisis.

Isabella Mayson was born in Milk Street, a busy little London thoroughfare with all the bustle and cries of a Charles Dickens B-movie. There was a corner pub, the Dolphin, drapers' shops running shoulder to shoulder with boot-

Sam Beeton

makers and butchers, and a noisy street market round the corner in Honey Lane. Most families in Milk Street lived 'over the shop', and Isabella and her three younger sisters were no exception.

Their mother, Elizabeth, a local printer's daughter, helped her husband Benjamin run his linen business. The living quarters and staircase, like those of their neighbours, would have been stacked with bolts of cloth. Milk Street was well known for its drapery shops, and Isabella would have spent her first few years clambering over fresh-smelling bales of Ulster linen and rolls of cambric. There was no easy money in the Cheapside cloth trade. Work was hard, heavy at times, and when Benjamin died at thirty-nine he left his twenty-five-year-old widow wondering how she could bring up her family.

Isabella was four years old at the time, and her mother, in desperation, wrote to Benjamin's father, a Cumberland clergyman, for money. The old man posted £50 which he had hoped to put on one side for his grandchildren later in life. Even in Victorian times the money was unlikely to go far; but Elizabeth had the good fortune to meet an ambitious Epsom printer called Henry Dorling. Their families had probably known each other in the printing trade and, as Henry was also a widower with four children, marriage seemed a practical solution to their problems.

The ceremony took place at Gretna Green where formalities were few in Victorian times. Elopement was certainly not the style of the rather pompous Mr Dorling, but the combination of a romantic and speedy union seemed appropriate. By all accounts it was a happy relationship, with an almost uninterrupted stream of thirteen more babies which filled the family home in Epsom High Street to bursting point.

The marriage turned Isabella's life upside down. She moved from their cramped quarters in Milk Street to a peaceful, prosperous life in the country. Tranquillity, however, was not quite the usual run of things. In mid-Victorian days, on Derby Day, Epsom came alive.

It was no accident that Dorling had settled there. The family, originally from Suffolk, ran a lucrative business printing Dorling's Genuine Card List, an early form card of runners and riders containing inside information on the day's races. It had first appeared at the 1827 Derby, touted round the course by a motley collection of misfits and one-eyed, one-legged eccentrics with such names as Donkey Jemmy, Sailor Jack and Fair Helen. Dorling's Correct Card, as it came to be known, was highly respected among racegoers and in great demand. It provided a steady income for Henry Dorling and, for a man with social ambitions, a perfect entrée to the well-heeled racing fraternity.

These early days in the white Georgian house in Epsom High Street made a great impression on young Isabella. The clattering machines, shouting stone-

Epsom High Street where Henry Dorling had his printing office.

hands and daily bustle of Dorling's Printing Office next door became familiar sights and sounds. Years later, when she moved into her own publishing offices in the Strand, the organized chaos of editing and production were to revive old memories. Many a Victorian lady would have found it unthinkable to inch her billowing skirt past dirty trays of type and wet page proofs, but for Isabella it was home. Journalists, they say, should feel equally at ease with dukes and dustmen, and life at Epsom proved a perfect training-ground for the future. Isabella loved talking to people – wherever she and Sam were to travel they would strike up conversations and friendships with all kinds of travellers on trains, ferries and buses. There is little doubt that the hurly-burly of the Epsom race-crowd provided her first taste for it.

On Derby Days the sleepy village, with its duck pond and handful of inns, was overrun with stage coaches, street entertainers, pie-sellers, confidence tricksters, aristocrats and horse trainers. Children swung on fences watching the strange caravan moving nose-to-tail through rural toll-gates for a day at the races. The return was usually more entertaining, with colliding coaches precipitating fights, drunken punters, shying horses and bedraggled travellers.

Isabella and her new family found themselves thrust into the midst of this seasonal circus. When Henry Dorling was appointed Clerk of the Course a house overrun with noisy children was unsuitable for conducting business. The offspring were moved from the High Street into the Grandstand. It was

How you travelled to the Victorian Derby depended very much on who you were.

a pillared, palatial affair, towering over the Downs and topped by an enormous Union Jack. For five shillings entrance fee a crowd of 5000 roared their favourites home from the slanting roof tier. Below were two floors containing living accommodation, four spacious restaurants, a ninety-foot saloon, retiring rooms for officials – even a travelling magistrate's court to deal with offenders on the spot. Henry and Elizabeth continued to live up at the house while the sprawling assortment of children had the run of the Grandstand, under the supervision of Isabella and a granny.

From the age of nine the smell of cooking drifted into Isabella's life from the huge kitchens in the basement of the Grandstand. It attracted Charles Dickens, too, when he visited the races in 1851. Henry Dorling showed him round, and Dickens was fascinated by the below-stairs army catering for thousands of racegoers. Later he described the scene in his magazine, *Household Words*:

> An exciting odour of cookery meets us in our descent. Rows of spits are turning rows of joints before blazing walls of fire. Cooks are trussing fowls; confectioners are making jellies; kitchen-maids are plucking pigeons; huge crates of boiled tongues are being garnished on dishes. One hundred and thirty legs of lamb, sixty-five saddles of lamb, and one hundred and thirty shoulders of lamb; in short a whole flock of sixty-five lambs have to be roasted and dished and garnished by Derby Day.
>
> Twenty rounds of beef, four hundred lobsters, one hundred and fifty tongues, twenty fillets of veal, one hundred sirloins of beef, five hundred spring chickens, three hundred and fifty pigeon pies; a countless number of quartern loaves, and an incredible quantity of ham have to be cut up into sandwiches; eight hundred eggs have got to be boiled for the pigeon-pies and salads. The forest of lettuces, the acres of cress, and the beds of radishes which will have to be chopped up; the gallons of dressing that will have to be poured out and converted into salads for the insatiable Derby Day will be best understood by a memorandum from the chief of that department to the chef-de-cuisine, which happened accidentally to fall under our notice: 'Pray don't forget a large tub and a birch broom for mixing the salad!'

A magical childhood for the girl who was later to give the world its favourite cookery book.

Henry Dorling held large dinner parties for friends and influential people, but generally was not regarded as a likeable man. Dickens was unimpressed by his self-importance, and among racegoers he was known as 'the dictator of Epsom'. Through years of dedicated social climbing he became a cornerstone of the racing establishment, and provided a solid, middle-class upbringing for his family, for whom he showed genuine affection.

Saddled with the responsibility of the children in the long months between race meetings, Isabella became a practical girl, perhaps a little old for her years, but with an impish sense of humour. A day-to-day awareness of household management was thrust upon her from an early age, cultivating in her an interest in cookery and, for a time, she took pastry lessons from a confectioner in Epsom High Street.

Henry Dorling's wealth and status enabled him to send Isabella to a superior school in Heidelberg, where she polished her French, music and cookery under the supervision of the proprietors, sisters Louisa and Auguste Heidel. She remained friendly with them for the rest of her life, and some German recipe suggestions from them were included in *Household Management*.

Samuel Beeton was also born in Milk Street, on the other side of the road from Isabella, just a few doors down at No. 39. His grandfather ran the Dolphin Tavern on the corner, where racing was always a great topic of conversation. The idea for the Publican's Derby at Epsom originated there.

Sam was sent to private school in Brentwood and, from an early age, became a voracious reader, cramming his head with any book which took his interest. By the time he arrived for his first job at a Fleet Street publishing house he was a thin, pale youth, full of ideas and creative energy. He became a fully-fledged working partner in Clarke, Beeton & Co, and lost no time finding his first bestseller.

It appeared in the form of Harriet Beecher Stowe's anti-slavery classic, *Uncle Tom's Cabin*. Harriet Beecher Stowe was deeply religious and believed that 'the Lord himself wrote it – I was but the humblest of instruments in his hand.' It was almost as if divine influence affected the sales, too: the book was snapped up at the rate of 1000 copies a week. Legally, Mrs Stowe was not entitled to royalties for British sales, but Sam Beeton felt that it was right that she should share in the book's success. In 1852 he sailed for America to meet the great lady herself, and to take the opportunity to make contact with Longfellow and Oliver Wendell Holmes.

Sam was impressed by American literature, and even more so by Harriet Beecher Stowe, a charming if rather serious lady. He was twenty-one, and she was the staid, middle-aged wife of a theologian. Despite this she was everything Sam considered a woman should be: intellectual, strong-willed and passionate

UNCLE TOM'S CABIN;

OR,

NEGRO LIFE

IN

THE SLAVE STATES OF AMERICA.

BY

HARRIET BEECHER STOWE.

With Forty Illustrations.

LONDON:
C. H. CLARKE AND CO., 148, FLEET STREET.

MDCCCLII.

Sam's first success —
Uncle Tom's Cabin.

in her fight for the under-privileged. America at that time buzzed with a naive optimism which strongly appealed to Sam's mercurial spirit. He instantly loved the earthy humour of Mark Twain and the direct, story-telling style of American books. After England, where publishing was over-priced, stuffy and conducted along the lines of a gentleman's club, America was like a breath of fresh air. Mrs Stowe epitomized everything Sam wished Englishwomen might be. He returned full of ideas and renewed enthusiasm for publishing, little knowing that he was soon to run into his own ideal woman in the shape of his cultured, capable childhood neighbour, Isabella Mayson.

Isabella's mother had kept in touch with her old friends from Milk Street, the Beetons. Both their children had moved from the unhealthy confines of the city to a new life in the country. Sam had always been slightly 'delicate', with early signs of chest trouble which was to dog him for the rest of his life. His mother had died when he was a toddler, and his grandmother had brought him up at Hadleigh. Like Isabella, closeted with the children in the Grandstand, he was not left entirely to his own devices. Sam's father kept in close touch and, impressed with the boy's appetite for reading, gave him the complete works of Shakespeare for his twelfth birthday.

By the time Isabella met him in London, where she went regularly for piano lessons, Sam was an urbane, literary man who instinctively appealed to her. His erratic health, not helped by his Fleet Street batchelor life, tugged strongly at her maternal instincts. By all accounts he changed little during his life apart from, under Isabella's influence, deepening his understanding of women. Later, even in sickness, he was still the boy-publisher, his restless, creative mind lighting up his face with ideas.

T. P. O'Connor, the exuberant publisher and parliamentarian, met Sam towards the end of his life. Even then, he was clearly still the same Sam Beeton Isabella had fallen in love with:

When you first saw him you were only conscious of a pair of eyes – large, brilliant, burning, a beautiful and almost dazzling blue-grey in colour. In some respects he might have stood for Don Quixote for, in addition to his phenomenal thinness, he wore his beard in a peculiar style. It was a beautiful grey – like the eyes – and it was brought down to a point just as is the typical beard of the Spaniard.

The intellect and the spirit of the man, however, shone as brightly as the eyes. He was a ferocious Radical; was a brilliant and fervent conversationalist, and often would talk to me for long hours together.

From the age of nineteen, the consumption Sam inherited from his mother began to worsen and give him trouble. Throughout their marriage Isabella was to worry about his spending long hours in the office and arriving home late. She nursed him and took care of him with a love and dedication he abundantly repaid. Life with Sam gave Isabella the freedom to be herself. Under his guidance and encouragement she became an independent adventuress, while remaining the sensitive, amusing girl who had stolen his heart. Their life together was to have many peaks and troughs, but their regard and respect for each other never changed.

The courtship of this unlikeliest of Victorian couples did not meet with wholehearted family approval. Henry Dorling had risen to dizzy heights in the titled, landowning world of the racing gentry. The rather Bohemian-looking, consumptive strip of a young man who published papers for women and boys was not his idea of a perfect partner for his step-daughter, but for most of the time he stifled his pride. Some of Isabella's sisters, who had depended on her so much for practical help, were not overjoyed at seeing her go. Typically in such situations, it was Isabella who took most of the pressure at home. The distance between Epsom and Bouverie Street did not help. Meetings were snatched over lunch at the Dolphin when Isabella went up to town for music lessons and, for a time, their relationship flourished by letter.

At Christmas 1855, when Sam's health had forced him to take a holiday in Suffolk, Isabella retreated from the family festivities to keep in touch:

Epsom
Dec 31st 1855

My dear Sam,
   . . . I was very glad to hear your cold was so much better, only mind and take care of yourself, as you promised you would, for I certainly was terribly afraid you were going to be seriously ill when I left you on Friday night . . . When I arrived home I found the girls had gone to Mr. Sherwood's to tea and turn out, so the old birds are quite alone.

   This week I do not come to town for a music lesson as I have not worked at all for him, also, as the children say, do not know my lesson, so it would be useless to come up. When do you start for Suffolk? I should like to know because then I can fancy what you are doing. Much to my annoyance I discovered this morning that I was invited to Mr. White's tomorrow evening, so I shall have to go through that terrible ordeal, a dinner party . . .

   Wish everybody a very happy New Year for me and tell your

sisters I hope they will spend a pleasant evening at Bow. John thinks of coming out in his tail-coat for the occasion. I am afraid he will look more like a monkey than a man; however, chacun a son gout.

Your affectionate Fatty,
Isabella

———————

Epsom
Jan 3rd 1856

My dear Sam,

. . . I cannot say I read your note with any degree of satisfaction; it was so full of the miserables. I was indeed sorry to hear you had been such a sufferer; now your enemy has departed you will be able to enjoy yourself in the country, and come back looking as jolly as a fat farmer. You know very well that is how I should like you to appear on your return.

. . . I hope you will not be offended with me for sending you a few envelopes: Father said this morning he supposed your passion for advertising was such that you could not resist sending these stamped affairs. Pray do not think me rude, but I cannot bear for all the world to know who my letter comes from. I can assure you I look upon your letters as far too sacred to lighten. That you will return in better health and think sometimes of somebody residing at Epsom, is the sincerest wish of your own

Isabella

———————

Once back behind his desk in Bouverie Street Sam lost no time in snatching a few moments to arrange to see Isabella again:

———————

London, Jan 31 1856

My dear Bella,

I am very delighted to think I am going to see you tomorrow, and can only say that I consider I owe a large debt of gratitude to my sisters, in prevailing on you to come to London, to Sig. Opertz' concert . . . You write 'you say' to ascertain my intentions – they are on this point as they always are on every matter connected with you (whom I prize and love beyond all other things) to do precisely and exactly as you wish. It will gratify me greatly to see you tomorrow, and if you can find means to let me know by what train you will arrive in town, I will meet you at London Bridge . . . If you can come up, dear Bella, tomorrow in time to go for a short walk with me, I shall be very glad, and if I can't hear from Epsom what time you will come to town, tell them at Milk Street to send down to Bouverie, the moment you are there, and on the wings of – but I had forgotten – no namby pamby nonsense, so dearest Bella, I am

    Yours with fondest love,
     S. O. Beeton

As the wedding approached in July that year, there was still clearly family friction which made Sam bridle. Isabella, caught in the middle, had to do her best to smooth things over:

Epsom
May 26 1856

My own darling Sam,

As I have two or three little matters in your note of yesterday which rather puzzled me, I thought I must write and ask an explanation; very stupid of me you will say, as I am going to see you on Wednesday morning, no doubt you will think I could just as well have my say then as trouble you with one of my unintelligible epistles.

In the first place, in what does Bella *sometimes now* pain Sam just a little? Why does he not wish to be near her? Secondly: what right has he to conjure up in his fertile imagination any such nasty things as rough corners to smooth down, when there is one who loves him better and more fondly than ever one being did another on *this* earth at least.

Oh Sam, I think it so wrong of you to fancy such dreadful things. You also say you don't think I shall be able to guide myself when I am left to my own exertions. I must certainly say I have always looked up to, and respected, both parents and perhaps been too mindful of what they say (I mean regarding certain matters), but then in a very short time you will have the entire management of me and I can assure you that you will find in me a most docile and willing pupil.

Pray don't imagine that when I am yours that things will continue the same way as they are now. God forbid. Better would it be to put an end to this matter altogether if we thought there was the slightest possibility of *that*, so pray don't tremble for our future happiness. Look at things in a more rosy point of view, and I have no doubt with the love I am sure there is existing between us we shall get on as merrily as crickets, with only an occasional sharp point to soften down, and not many, as you fancy.

I am very tired indeed tonight, as I have been at the Stand all day long, and of course have not sat down all day. I wish I had you near me that I might just love you a very little bit. On Wednesday you will have a nice talk with me and can tell me all about matters; I certainly wish they were come to a conclusion. I could not sleep without writing to you, so you must excuse this nonsense. Good night, my precious pet, may angels guard and watch over you and give you pleasant dreams, not drab colours, and accept the fondest and most sincere love of,

Your devoted
Bella Mayson
Burn this as soon as perused.

———————

Her words clearly soothed Sam's pre-marital nerves, as he replied:

———————

Bouverie
Tuesday afternoon

My dearest Bella,

. . . You're a dear little brick, and blessed must have been the earth of which you were baked. I could not find the slightest speck of a fault in any one of your remarks, for there exists no one more mindful of the respect and love due to a parent than your cavaliero, who is now writing to you.

Well, my own loved one, you have made me so much happier and more comfortable today as I see you write so firmly, yet so prettily, upon that dreaded subject of interference, that now I do quite hope that matters will not remain as they now are. I don't desire, I assure you, to manage you – you can do that quite well yourself – my only desire, my sweetest darling, is that no one else should manage you. You, as you know, can do anything with me . . . I have written you this with many people in and out of the office, so if anything is particularly absurd, consider it not there.

S.O.B.

———————

The wedding took place at Epsom parish church with a lavish reception in the Grandstand, organized with all the pomp and occasion the Clerk of the Course could muster. *The Times* carried the announcement:

On the 10th inst. at Epsom by the Rev. B. Bradney Brocket, vicar, Samuel Orchart Beeton Esq., of Bouverie St., and Pinner, Middlesex, eldest son of the late Samuel Powell Beeton Esq., of Milk Street, City, to Isabella Mary Mayson, eldest daughter of the late Benjamin Mayson Esq., of Milk St.

As the carriage pulled away down the racecourse, leaving the huddle of well-dressed guests waving from the Grandstand steps, Sam and Isabella obviously sighed with relief that it was over. Isabella had no fears for the traditional ordeal, the Victorian honeymoon. They were deeply in love and felt that together they had overcome the odds. At the end of three weeks in Europe she returned home happy and pregnant to a new life in Pinner.

Their first son, named Samuel Orchart after his father, was born the following year. Isabella was translating French novels for the *Englishwoman's Domestic Magazine*, and had embarked on *Household Management* by the time the baby arrived. Three months later, still finding it hard to regain her strength, she left Pinner for a short visit to Newmarket to stay with a friend, Mrs English. While she was away from home, the baby developed the croup – a wracking cough associated with choking – and died.

Infant death was common at the time, and the rather cloying sentimentality with which Victorians surrounded it showed that it was not entirely unexpected. Isabella, nevertheless, was devastated. Sam gave all his support but was deeply shaken. A month went by in which her usual work for the magazine failed to appear. Then, as an indication of her resolute character, Mrs Beeton submerged herself in *Household Management* with a dedication and thoroughness sharpened by tragedy.

Two years later – in the middle of the four-years' research on her kitchen classic – their second child was born. He, too, was called Samuel Orchart, and appeared a strong, healthy child. The Beetons, overworked but on the threshold of new, exciting ventures, found the baby just the tonic they needed. Life at Pinner took on a fresh dimension. Sam's reputation was growing. He was on the point of launching the *Boy's Penny Magazine* and the first *Christmas Annual*, while Isabella had broken the back of her enormous book. They held lively dinner parties at Chandos Villa which friends remembered for good food and a wealth of wit and conversation – quite unlike the formal ordeals faced by some of the women readers of their magazine.

Sam's hugely successful boys' magazine was a major stepping-stone in his publishing career.

THE

BOY'S OWN VOLUME

OF

Fact, Fiction, History, and Adventure.

MIDSUMMER, 1863.

ILLUSTRATED BY

SEPARATE PLATES,

AND NUMEROUS WOODCUTS INSERTED IN THE TEXT.

EDITED BY THE PUBLISHER.

LONDON:
S. O. BEETON, 248, STRAND, W.C.

When the baby was six months old and thriving, Sam and Isabella took a short working holiday to Ireland. They left Euston at 9.00 p.m. for Holyhead and, after travelling all night, boarded the S.S. *Llewllyn* at Holyhead at 5.00 a.m. the following day. The steam packet, like its sister ship the *St Columba*, had been commissioned by the Admiralty to service the new boat trains chugging regularly into Anglesey. The sea lay like a millpond beneath a blanket of thick fog. A few hours later, as the *Llewllyn* cautiously nosed its way towards Dublin, there was a tremendous crash as they hit a sand bar off Howth Island.

Isabella, who had been sitting on deck in the eerie silence before the boat erupted into pandemonium, calmly recorded in her diary; 'Ran aground off Howth Island. Fortunately more frightened than hurt. Sea very calm.' The *Llewllyn* eventually freed itself and steamed uncertainly up the Liffey. 'Nearly left our luggage behind,' she added. 'Arrived in Dublin, went to Jury's Hotel, College Green, very comfortable quarters. After washing and making ourselves comfortable had breakfast and walked into Phoenix Park along the banks of the Liffey.'

It was an idyllic fortnight, providing a much-needed rest, and Sam and Isabella enjoyed it with the abandon of two children on a school outing. They rode the winding Irish lanes in jaunting cars, and spent hours listening to tales of Irish legends from the locals. They made their base in the tranquillity of Killarney, at the Railway Hotel near the lake. It was there, between paddling

Gt. Southern Hotel. Killarney.

The Railway Hotel, Killarney, in Mrs Beeton's day.

Even on the Railway Hotel's centenary the dining room had changed little from the days of Sam and Isabella's holiday. Today it stands disused and empty.

and scrambling up hills, they celebrated their fourth wedding anniversary.

One day they rowed up the Long Range, a gentle trout stream, and Isabella later recalled in her pocket book: 'Landed and made our way up the mountain to the Gap of Dunloe. Girls with bare feet carrying goat's milk tormented us to buy of them. Very be-ringed handsome girls with smart shawls over their heads. Danced on the Lady's Rest to a very peculiar wild air . . .'

Predictably, it poured for days – 'a bit of damp weather,' as the Irish say – and the time was passed preparing articles for the *Englishwoman's Domestic Magazine*. Sam answered readers' problem letters, while Isabella made travel notes for future features.

They returned somewhat reluctantly to London, relaxed, but not without a little anxiety. Publication day was looming for the first book version of *Household Management*, and Isabella was understandably apprehensive about its reception. Sam, as usual, was looking two steps to the future. He had already had a hand in launching the *Sporting Life*, and was now working on a topical women's weekly called the *Queen*, which still flourishes as *Harpers & Queen*.

Isabella's worries were unfounded. *Household Management* achieved the great success it deserved. The Beeton partnership was running at full strength, but it did little to prepare them for a further family disaster.

After five years at Pinner – a house full of memories, which had seen them

The Beeton's imposing office near the Law Courts in the Strand.

arrive in uncertainty from honeymoon and rise together to the peak of their careers – the lease ran out. After rented accommodation, however grand, Sam and Isabella felt they would like to buy a house of their own. To give themselves time to browse the lists of vacant properties, they moved 'over the shop' into a temporary flat above their offices in the Strand.

London air did little to improve Sam's persistent, hacking cough, which worsened as the damp winter weather closed in. They decided to spend Christmas in Brighton where, as Victorians believed, the ozone billowed in bracingly from the sea. They took baby Samuel Orchart, now three, along with them. Just after the Christmas celebrations he developed a rash, which Isabella identified with great alarm as scarlet fever. His condition worsened over the next few days and, as the hotel broke into its New Year's Eve revelries, Samuel died.

Sam's stepmother purchased a family plot big enough for three graves at Norwood Cemetery for the little boy's funeral, little knowing that both Isabella and Sam would be laid to rest there alongside him within a few years. Isabella, who, ironically, had written the definitive work on making a home and bringing up children, now found herself with neither.

THE BEETON TRACK

Slowly they picked up the pieces again and decided to make a fresh start. They bought an idyllic country villa, Mount Pleasant, at Greenhithe. It lay on the Thames on a picturesque rise, long since bulldozed to make way for a cement factory. There, surrounded by roses, honeysuckle, an old mare and a donkey, they created a rural retreat. In the summertime, it was a haven of blossom and sleepy bees and, amid such relaxing charm, Isabella discovered that she was pregnant again.

The baby was another boy, Orchart, born on the first anniversary of their second child's death. The baby showed no signs of ill-health, and Isabella plunged herself once more into running the editorial side of the business. She visited Paris to oversee the fashion plates for the *Englishwoman's Domestic Magazine*, and was soon delighted to find herself, at the age of twenty-eight, expecting a fourth child. She joined Sam on a business trip to Berlin before returning to Greenhithe to await the birth.

They were both hard at work on a new publication called the *Young Englishwoman*, equally sharing the duties of preparing it for publication. Sam, staying briefly at Newmarket that year, dropped a brief note to Isabella which shows how technically proficient she had become, as well as how much in love they were still:

Send the description of the eight pages you have already got up for the Young Englishwoman as soon as pos' with the cliches to Cox and Wyman, and ask C.W. to let Poulter do the making up. This done, the next thing is the sheet of Dble Demy with two sets of diagrams and needlework patterns, given us, that is to say, the suppt for the Young E'Woman for two weeks . . . Goodbye my girl, sweet kisses on thy fair-formed brow I'd give, but can't just now.

It was a joyful Christmas and, with the launch of the magazine over, Isabella began work on the proofs of a new book, the *Dictionary of Cookery*. She abandoned it only when the first labour pains began on 29 June 1865. Later that day, their fourth son, Mayson, was born.

Sam and Isabella were understandably happy, especially at the sight of young Orchart toddling in to inspect the new arrival. But by the following morning Sam was showing concern. Isabella was feverish and very unwell. A doctor was quickly called and diagnosed puerperal fever. There was a reasonable chance Isabella would recover, and Sam spent all his time at her bedside. She clung on for a week as her temperature raged, and then Sam watched his beloved Isabella die.

87

His agony, as he said in a letter to a relative, was 'a dreadful grief that well nigh overpowers me and renders me unable to move or stir'.

He stumbled through the motions of going to the office and looking after his two young sons. When the *Dictionary of Cookery* was published he publicly revealed his feelings at the loss of his devoted partner and greatest friend:

USQUE AD FINEM

Her hand has lost its cunning – the firm true hand that wrote these formulae and penned the information contained in this little book. Cold in the silent tomb lie the once nimble, useful fingers – now nerveless, unable for anything, and ne'er to do work more in this world. Exquisite palate, unerring judgement, sound common sense, refined tastes – all these had this dear lady who has gone 'ere her youth had scarcely come. But four times seven years were all she passed in this world; and since the day she became wedded wife – now nearly nine years past – her greatest, chiefest aims were to provide for the comfort and pleasure of those she loved and had around her, and to employ her best faculties for the use of her sisters, Englishwomen generally. Her surpassing affection and devotion led her to find happiness in aiding with all her heart and soul, the Husband whom she richly blessed and honoured with her abounding love.

Her works speak for themselves; and although taken from this world in the very height of her health and strength, and in the early days of womanhood, she felt the satisfaction – so great to all who strive with good intent and warm will – of knowing herself regarded with respect and gratitude.

Her labours are ended here, in purer atmosphere she dwells; and maybe in the land beyond the skies, she has a nobler work to accomplish. Her plans for the future cannot be wholly carried out; her husband knew them all, and will diligently devote himself to their execution, as far as may be. The remembrance of her wishes – always for the private and public welfare – and her companionship of her two little boys – too young to know the virtues of their good mother – this memory, this presence, will nerve the Father, left alone, to continue to do his duty; in which he will follow the example of his wife, for her duty no woman has ever better accomplished than the late

ISABELLA MARY BEETON

The Epsom raceday circus which left a lasting impression on young Isabella. The Grandstand, where she lived with her brothers and sisters, towers in the background.

The Victorian nursery – often tucked away in a remote corner of the house. Children were preferably neither seen nor heard.

The Beeton family grave at Norwood, where Sam and Isabella lie together.

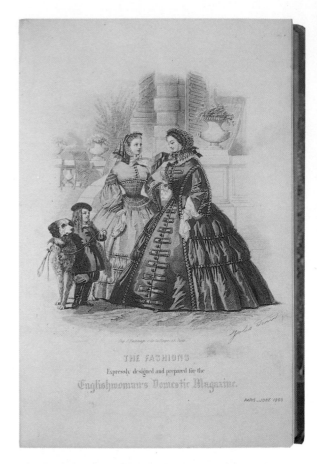

A selection of colour plates from the *Englishwoman's Domestic Magazine*.

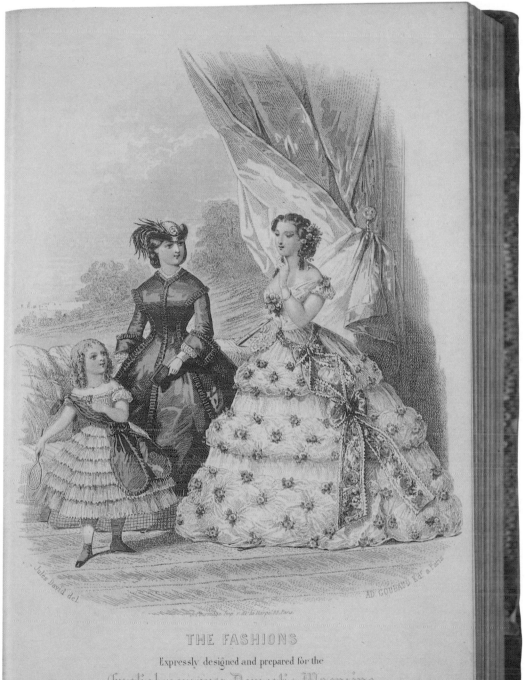

Jules David del.

Imp. Burgeaud Imp. r. de la Harpe. 23. Paris.

AD. GOUBAUD Edr à Paris

THE FASHIONS

Expressly designed and prepared for the

Englishwoman's Domestic Magazine.

SEPTEMBER 1860

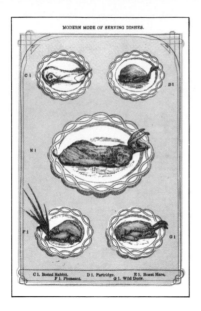

C 1. Boiled Rabbit.   D 1. Partridge.   E 1. Roast Hare.
F 1. Pheasant.   G 1. Wild Duck.

N 1. Raised Pie.   O 1. Vol-au-Vent.   P 1. Christmas Plum Pudding in Mould.
Q 1. Apples in Custard.   R 1. Charlottes aux Pommes.

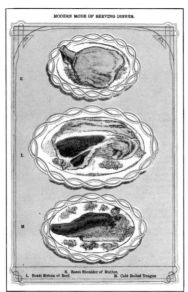

K. Roast Shoulder of Mutton.
L. Roast Sirloin of Beef.   M. Cold Boiled Tongue.

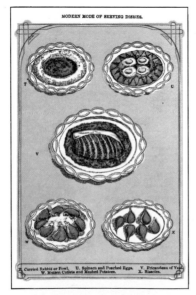

T. Curried Rabbit or Fowl.   U. Spinach and Poached Eggs.   V. Fricandeau of Veal.
W. Mutton Cutlets and Mashed Potatoes.   X. Rissoles.

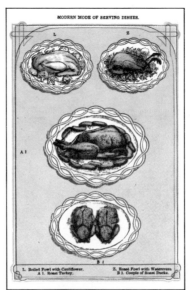

L. Boiled Fowl with Cauliflower.   Z. Roast Fowl with Watercress.
A 1. Roast Turkey.   B 1. Couple of Roast Ducks.

H. Dressed Lobster.   G. Scalloped Oysters.   I. Dressed Crab.

A selection of colour plates from the first edition of *Household Management*.

6
The Englishwoman's Domestic Magazine

Women's magazines, and publishing in general, owe a lot to the prolific Beetons. From beneath the sign of the beehive came *Boy's Own Magazine*, *Queen* (now *Harper's & Queen*), the first Christmas annuals, the first partworks which readers bought each week and collected, handicraft books, fiction and dictionaries of universal information. It was a production line of popular journalism, cleverly aimed at vast sections of Victorian society who had little of real interest to read.

Sam Beeton made his name publishing the first British edition of *Uncle Tom's Cabin*, but the cornerstone of the business was the *Englishwoman's Domestic Magazine*. From the outset, when it first appeared on the news-stands in 1852, it was clearly very different from any other woman's magazine of the day. Sam, a natural radical, had a good instinct for what thousands of housebound women would enjoy: good fiction, advice pages, gardening, cookery and fashion. All the ingredients, in short, of today's successful women's publications.

The *Englishwoman's Domestic Magazine* set many of the standards and, with the skills of Mrs Beeton, circulation exceeded their expectations. It was also one of the first publications to offer a 'prize raffle' – the forerunner of newspaper bingo – with gold watches and chains for the winners. In its early years Sam gave away more than 3000 guineas-worth as a circulation-booster.

1859 saw the greatest changes and adventures in the Beetons' short time together. Sam moved from his cramped offices in Bouverie Street to a prestigious building near the Law Courts in the Strand. Their second child, baby Samuel Orchart, was born in the autumn and, after two years of extremely hard work, *Household Management* was advertised for the first time as a partwork. Although it was another two years before Mrs Beeton's kitchen classic appeared in book form, Sam and Isabella were deep in discussion drawing up plans to expand their magazine interests. They both felt that fashion was a growing market and Isabella, now confident of her writing ability, put on a new hat and launched into fashion journalism.

The idea of a regular column on women's and children's wear was nothing new – the *Englishwoman's Domestic Magazine* had featured a rather drab piece for years with black and white illustrations. But the Beetons, as usual, wanted to take the magazine industry by surprise. Journal publishing was, if anything, perhaps even more competitive in those days than today, with new magazines appearing almost weekly. Sam had fought hard to retain a loyal readership and, with Isabella's flair, was poised to revolutionize the *Englishwoman's Domestic Magazine* with a huge circulation drive.

The magazine's somewhat jaded feature, the 'Practical Dress Instructor', was popular, but generally uninspired. The Beetons wanted to move upmarket, and considered it unlikely to attract the readership of middle-class women whose appetite for fashion was more sophisticated.

They discussed the problem with Madame Roche, who contributed general fashion news, and decided to launch a series of colour plates of the latest Paris fashions, with the added attraction of dress patterns which readers could purchase by post from the magazine. It seemed a sure-fire winner, and Sam and Isabella left the baby with nanny and set off for Paris to make the arrangements.

The late Nancy Spain, who was related to the Beetons, wrote in her biography of them in 1948:

> The idea of a young Englishwoman of the middle classes, on hands and knees in the front parlour, pinning and cutting out a crinoline from a vast bale of silk would have been ludicrous to anyone but the practical and revolutionary Isabella. She was enchanted. Sam, pacing restlessly up and down, worked out his scheme financially. It would be expensive, but provided that a large enough number were cut, it would work.

Crochet Bonnet.

(A) *Flower in middle of Crown.*—7 chain, make it round, "1 s.c., 5 chain, repeat four times more," * 10 chain, turn, miss 1, 1 d.c., 2 long, 3 d long, 2 long, 1 d.c.; * 1 s.c. in 3rd chain; 1 s.c. in 4th chain stitch; 5 chain, join to 3rd d. long; 10 chain, join to the point of same section, turn, "4 chain, 1 s.c., repeat twice more." Then work same as on 10 chain. 1 s.c. in 5 chain. Repeat on the other four 5 chain, as on this. See the bud. 1 s.c. between 1st and 2nd section of *A*, 15 chain, turn, miss 5; 1 s.c. in 6th and in round loop, "1 s.c., 6 chain; turn, 1 d.c., 3 long, 1 d.c. repeat four times more." Then down the stem 3 s.c., 3 d.c., 3 s.c.; fasten off. Work 4 more *B*'s between each section of *A*.

(B) * 1 s.c. in 2nd section of 1st bud, 4 chain; 1 s.c. in 3rd section, 4 chain; 1 s.c. in 4th section: 9 chain, 1 s.c. in 2nd section of 4 chain, at the top of *A*; 9 chain, repeat 4 times more *, 1 long in each chain, stitch, fasten off.

(C) 5 chain, make it round; "1 s.c., 5 chain, repeat 5 times more," * 1 s.c., in 1st chain of 5 chain; 7 chain, turn, miss 1, 1 d.c., 1 long, 2 d. long, 1 long, 1 d.c., 1 s.c. in 2nd chain, 1 s.c. in 3rd chain stitch; 3 chain, join to 2nd d. long of last section; 8 chain, join to the top of same section; "1 s.c., 3 chain, repeat twice more," miss 1, work on chain, same as on 7 chain. Repeat 5 times more * each C, as you work it. Join to the long stitches; work sufficient number to go round the long stitches.

(D) 13 chain, join to C, repeat all round, making it lay quite easy to the shape. 2nd row—d.c. on each chain. 3rd row—1 s.c. on 1st d.c. stitch, "11 chain, miss 6; 1 s.c. in 7th d.c., 7 chain; 1 s.c. in same d.c., 11 chain, 1 s.c. in same d.c., 7 chain, 1 s.c. in same d.c., repeat all round;" fasten off. 4th row—1 s.c. in 6th chain of 11 chain, repeat as in 3rd row, only mind that you bring the plain 11 chain over the tuft in last row; fasten off.

(E) 14 chain, make it round, 5 d.c., 1 s.c. in 4th chain of 7 chain of D, 5 d.c., 1 s.c. in 6th chain of 11 chain of D, 14 d.c.; fasten off.

(F) 12 chain, make it round, 28 long in round loop, "7 chain, miss 3, 1 s.c. in 4th long, repeat 7 times more," 9 d.c. round each 7 chain; join each as you work them. Work another row of F; join as seen in engraving.

(G) 5 chain, make it round, 8 d.c. in round loop, "5 chain, miss 1, 1 s.c. in next loop, repeat 3 times more;" fasten off. Join each G between the two rows of G.

(H) 20 chain, turn, miss 7, and in 8th 1 s.c., 12 d.c. "5 chain, miss 1; 1 s.c., repeat 5 times more." D.c. round each 5 chain. Down the stem 5 s.c., 3 d.c., turn; up the stem again 3 s.c.: 27 chain, "turn, 5 long, 1 d.c., 1 s.c.," 9 chain, turn, 5 long; 1 d.c., 1 s.c., "8 chain, same as 9 chain, 3 s.c., down the stem;" same as 9 chain, 3 s.c. down the stem; same as 8 chain, 6 s.c. down the stem; pass the hook underneath, 1 s.c. on the other side; 18 chain, miss 7, 1 s.c. in 8th stitch then in round loop 11 d.c., down the stem 4 s.c.; 6 d.c., 4 s.c., 9 d.c., repeat from * till sufficient length. Work another row of F, joining to H, as in engraving.

(I) 7 chain, make round, and work 10 d.c.; fasten off.

(K) Make a chain, joining, as you make it, to I and F, of sufficient length; fasten off. 2nd row —5 chain, miss 4, 1 s.c. in 5th repeat. 3rd row—on 1st s.c. *, 15 chain, miss 2, 5 chain, 1 s.c. on 1 s.c., "11 chain, 1 s.c., 15 chain, 1 s.c., 11 chain, 1 s.c., all in same 1 s.c., repeat all round *. 4th row—* 1 s.c. on 8th stitch of 15 chain, 11 chain, 1 s.c., 15 chain, 1 s.c., 11 chain on same stitch, 15 chain, 1 s.c. in 8th stitch of 15 chain; 15 chain, repeat from *. Repeat 3rd and 4th rows till wide enough for the shape.

(L) 4 chain, miss 2, 1 s.c. in 3rd all round, and in each 4 chain, 5 d.c.

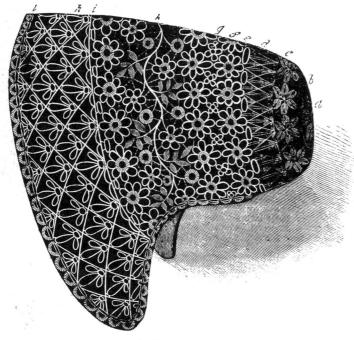

CROCHET BONNET.

Embroidery.

Applique.

Silk Patchwork.

English Embroidery.

Knitting.

93

As they talked Isabella feverishly worked out the arithmetic in a little pocket diary she always carried. Almost a century later Nancy Spain discovered it among bundles of family papers:

	£	s.	d.
Paper for 4to pp	3	10	0
Working do.	0	15	0
Fashions	2	0	0
Arabe	3	0	0
Patron paper	1	0	0
Working do.	0	7	0
	£10	12	0
Returns .... £15 0 0 per thousand			
Composition	18	0	0
Editing	15	0	0
Engravings	10	0	0
	£43	0	0

12,000 just pays.

Many women would, of course, never have dreamed of kneeling down and cutting out their own dresses, but, in the days before television and instant international news reporting, the prospect of wearing up-to-date Paris fashions was too much to resist. Small dressmaking shops suddenly found themselves innundated with requests to make up designs from the mail-order patterns on fawn patron paper, sent in exchange for forty-two one-penny stamps.

Sam and Isabella had arranged to see Adolphe Goubaud, the French publisher of *Le Moniteur de la Mode*, one of several Paris magazines using colour fashion plates. His offices were in the Rue de Richelieu, a few blocks from the Bibliothèque Nationale.

While Sam drew up the business deal, Isabella was taken to the workrooms, two streets away in bustling Rue Sainte Anne. Later she recorded in her tiny diary: 'The director took me over the workroom, saw the girls colouring the various fashion plates. Gentleman offered to send me home in his carriage.'

From labouring on *Household Management* in the kitchen at Pinner, she was finally spreading her wings and emerging as a confident businesswoman and writer, whose judgment Sam not only trusted but increasingly relied upon. Part of the arrangement included a regular news bulletin on the latest fashions sent by Madame Goubaud. With the help of these first-hand observations, Isabella launched into her new role as though she were reporting from the fashion houses and strolling the boulevards on behalf of her readers.

Our Practical Dress Instructor.

306 OUR PRACTICAL DRESS INSTRUCTOR.

Fig.1
BACK

Fig.2
FRONT

A

A

COLLAR

HALF of SLEEVE

DIAGRAMS OF BOY'S DRESS.
Fig. 1. Back. Fig. 2. Front : A to A to fold back, for in-door dress. Collar to fix on out-door dress.

The Boy's Dress here shown is very generally worn, both in and out of the house. Velvet or cloth are the materials of which it is composed; and the Belt is a patent leather one.

The Lady's Dress, and the Diagrams which compose it, will be given in our next Number.

Isabella blossomed under the freedom and independence she had longed for so much during her courtship, and decided to work from the office in the Strand. Sam the idealist pushed the image of the New Woman in his pages, but Isabella, at twenty-four, strong and cultured, quietly went about living it. In fashion, as in cookery, she wrote with authority and conviction, attacking the subject in a highly technical style which presumably left her readers in awe. Here at last was an opportunity not only to read at first hand about high fashion but, for a moderate sum, to wear it too.

Magazine sales rocketed and Isabella, like Sam, adapted to the changes with vigour and enthusiasm. They became equal parts of the same whole, united in ambition and a genuine love for each other. The detail and arrangements of the profitable Paris venture had been difficult to set up, but in the hands of a formidable organizer like Mrs Beeton, they proved a runaway success. Thanks to the 3s. 6d patterns, and increased circulation, the cover price of the *Englishwoman's Domestic Magazine* was raised to sixpence.

Isabella visited Paris once a year to maintain her contact with the Goubauds, and visit the print workshops. Her own fashion tastes changed with those of the magazine, and she acquired a fondness for sophisticated, expensively-cut dresses. Mrs Beeton appeared to believe her own idiom – no matter how strange the latest designs, no one looked quite so out of place as those who did not wear them. By today's standards her fashion articles make heavy reading, but many a provincial heart must have leapt at the idea of black and white net Zouave jackets, or the shimmer of glacé silk.

Isabella's talents became indispensable to the business. She helped with a correspondence column, giving witty replies to the bulging bag of letters. In May 1860, the issue in which the first fashion plate appeared, she advised an anxious 'Emma E.':

You like, of course to be 'in fashion'. No young lady of sense and position wishes to be unlike her sisters and her cousins. It isn't in human nature that she should. In reply to your query respecting bonnets, we have to say that the reign of small bonnets is extinct; that dynasty is dethroned to give way to much longer-sized ones, which come considerably forward over the head, and have a somewhat 'coal-scuttle' appearance in front, while the back of the bonnet is composed of a 'loose crown'. So, if a young gentleman given to punning asks you to lend him five shillings, you can't now be able to reply that you haven't a loose crown about you. Mothers, therefore, beware!

The great success of the *Englishwoman's Domestic Magazine* was making news. The *Standard* ran a special feature which concluded:

It is but sixpence, and for that tiny coin Mr Beeton provides forty-eight pages of excellent matter . . . and outlines of the newest fashions, so that ladies may, if they please, have their dresses made up at home by a girl 'coming in'. We have the authority of 'materfamilias' for saying that the house would go to sixes and sevens if the magazine failed to put in its monthly appearance.

Sam took advantage of the Victorians' love of letter-writing by encouraging women to drop a line to the magazine about anything which came into their heads. Like all good editors he was astute enough to realize that the correspondence page was the barometer of the magazine's success. Dissatisfaction with stories could be anticipated at an early stage, and readers' interests which had perhaps never occurred to him quickly catered for. Inevitably many of the letters were about personal problems. Social conventions made it difficult for middle-class women to turn to anyone for help and advice, least of all their husbands. In the years before he married Isabella, Sam's answer to this growing need was to launch the forerunner of the modern agony column, 'Cupid's Letter Bag'. The innovation was, we can safely assume, a source of private amusement, as his mischievous replies to some of the more naive letters show:

LAURA B. (Camden Town) – 'I have two lovers and know not which to choose. One is rich, and has given me several handsome presents; the other is poor, but so attentive and kind that I feel he would make the best husband. I have been brought up in every comfort, and dread poverty, so know not how to decide.'

–LAURA'S LETTER is certainly very businesslike, and betrays but little genuine love for either of her admirers. For the sake of the poor lover, however, who really may be silly enough to value affection, we would advise her by all means to marry his richer rival, as like 'Pamela' the 'gilt coach and Flanders' mare' has evidently its attractions for Laura.

CUPID'S LETTER-BAG.

LAVINA CLOTILDA (Copenhagen) – 'A young man whom I love and who used, when he lived in the same town, to be very kind to me, will now when he occasionally comes, pass me in the street without looking or speaking. What shall I do?'

–FORGET HIM as soon as possible.

ROSE-BUD – 'I want to know if there is any harm in sending a present to a gentleman, merely inclosing it in an envelope, without signing my name?'

–WE CONSIDER the sending a present to a gentleman, under any circumstances, a doubtful proceeding, and only to be tolerated if he is a friend of the family, or engaged to the lady. Rose-Bud must remember that men are vain creatures, and apt to construe small attentions into great encouragement.

Occasionally the *Englishwoman's Domestic Magazine* received letters from men. While some expressed fury at feminist opinions expressed between the covers, others took advantage of the readership to appeal for a partner:

W.A.C. – 'A young man, 26, is not aware if he is good-looking, and anyway does not care whether he is or not. Has some small property, and has a situation in Somerset House and can muster perhaps a sum not under £250 per annum. He writes to Cupid for a nice, neat, natty amiable little girl, under twenty; fair, good-looking, plenty of ringlets and no affectation about her. One who can waltz and make pies. No crochet-workers need be recommended.'

When a man's vision of heaven is a pretty girl who can waltz and make pies, one can only hope he found the woman of his dreams.

The more mature readership of the revamped *Englishwoman's Domestic Magazine* was not as easily titillated by the breathless questions of 'Cupid's Letter Bag'. Eventually the column was dropped and replaced by the less frivolous 'Englishwoman's Conversazione'. The replies were as witty as ever, though the overall tone was more serious. Sam continued to use the page to push his progressive ideas of greater independence and education for women, though he was rather intolerant of the more simpering correspondents:

HELEN – We would rather not give our opinion on the subject of which you write; but physicians do say that red noses are among the injurious effects of tight lacing. A word to the prudent is enough!

Isabella occasionally lent a hand at the letters desk. Some of her replies, particularly to young girls, were extremely sympathetic and touching. Unlike Sam, who had a universal affection for women, Mrs Beeton did not suffer fools so gladly:

AN APPEAL – Can any of our readers aid the inquiring EVA SINCLAIR? She says she will feel obliged to the editor if he will inform her of the composition of the cosmetic used in the time of Charles the Second by the beauties of the Court, which really had the power of calling the crimson stream of the blood to the exterior fibres of the cheeks, and producing a beautiful rosy colour like unto the bloom of nature itself.

–WE think the use of water and friction – why should we not at once say, a good wash – cannot be equalled for MISS SINCLAIR's purpose. But some of our readers will come to EVA's rescue possibly with a more philosophic remedy.

Or the equally acerbic:

> CONSTANCE MADELINE may rest assured that her letters to us
> are never tampered with. We have had no opportunity, ere this, of
> answering her questions. It is not difficult to tell what 'will render
> the complexion a *dead* white.' Anything that would take away life
> itself would effect this object. But as life, if not ruddy health, is
> evidently precious to our – we suppose we cannot say *fair* –
> correspondent, she may resort to any of the following expedients for
> destroying the 'brilliant colour' in a maiden's cheeks, and here is a
> choice of them: Eat, fasting every other day, for about three months,
> a few sticks of slate pencil, or the stems of some new tobacco pipes;
> but should this be too arduous a task, then instead eat two or three
> tablespoons of flour, three or four times a day, for five or six weeks,
> and the countenance will gradually assume the aspect of – a person
> just recovering from jaundice.

Letters to the 'Englishwoman's Converzatione' also reflected the success of
the practical needlework pages. Crochet, embroidery, knitting and appliqué
work were featured each month with simple instructions printed beneath the
design.

> E.P. BYRNE should not write us an angry letter because we had not,
> last month, space sufficient to tell her that we would soon give a
> pattern for a 'night-dress'. Have patience; the building of Rome was
> not done in a day.

The excitement the magazine generated among ladies made the readership,
at times, seem like a class of unruly schoolgirls. The handicraft pages were one
of the journal's lasting successes.

From the style of some of the articles it would seem that Mrs Beeton
contributed to 'Receipts for Cookery' and 'The Sickroom and Nursery'. As she
assumed more control of the *Englishwoman's Domestic Magazine* various regular
features were dropped as the hard core of middle-class readers grew. Among
them was one of Sam's inventions, the 'Sybilline Interpreter', which lay half-

way between a horoscope and an agony column. Readers had to choose a number from 'The Sybil' and their questions would be answered. It was entertaining for those who took part, but probably of lesser interest to general readers.

Both Sam and Isabella worked long hours and, as with most journalists, even holidays were combined with business trips. Because of this, rather than despite it, their relationship grew closer. Sam's health had never been good but, with Isabella's energy and endless enthusiasm, the ideas continued to flow. Copies of the *Englishwoman's Domestic Magazine* can be tracked down today only in a handful of specialist antiquarian bookshops, but its influence is still evident whenever we open the pages of a women's magazine.

7

A Woman's Place . . .

Mrs Beeton and Her 'Sisters'

The roles of Victorian middle-class men and women were very clearly defined, and so rooted that traces of them can still be seen today. Men went out to work while women stayed at home, managing the house and bringing up children. The influence of these values was so strong that, even a hundred and fifty years later, there are married couples who feel uncomfortable deviating from them. A Victorian woman's place was firmly in the home, though this, of course, did not prevent her having her own opinions on men in general, more often than not expressed in drawing-room gossip. Nevertheless, women as a whole tended to accept their lot.

Some suffered terribly at the hands of violent husbands, as a selection of correspondence from the *Englishwoman's Domestic Magazine*'s letter-bag shows. There was, at the same time, a growing desire by battered wives to discover what rights, if any, they had in law:

MARY H. – We are happy to tell you that it is now illegal for a husband to strike or beat his wife. His right of 'moderate correction' was first questioned in the time of Charles the Second, and is now indefensible. A wife has right to the custody of her child up to seven years of age. The personal property of the wife passes to her husband absolutely on her marriage, but her real (ie. freehold) property can only be alienated by him during her life with her consent. A wife may demand maintenance from her husband, but cannot pledge his credit even for necessaries, if she would voluntarily quit his protection.

Sam and Isabella, fortunate to have an unusually close relationship, were deeply sympathetic of the plight of women trapped in harrowing marriages. From our viewpoint it is easy to wonder why women endured such indignity for so long, but many face similar problems today – only attitudes have changed. A battered Victorian wife would find it more difficult to get support and understanding if she walked out on her husband. The home was a shrine to everything middle-class family life represented. For a woman to take the first step towards breaking it up would have been considered a cardinal sin. Men were allowed their indiscretions, but a woman's lot was regulated by countless unspoken conventions and social attitudes.

As their replies show, the Beetons genuinely wanted to help unhappy wives and, perhaps motivated by their own singular characters, advised some to leave. It was unusual, almost sensational advice, but well received by thousands of women who read the magazine with great interest. One letter, quite long by letter-bag standards, was answered by Sam. Despite modern social and statistical studies of the Victorian era, there is nothing quite so human, or indeed revealing, as the pages of a popular journal:

Children were paraded at suitable occasions for the satisfaction of grown-ups.

A WIFE.– Mr. Editor, can you tell me how to manage an unkind husband? But, since there are so many forms of unkindness, I must tell you of what I complain. It is now about two years since I was married. A month had scarcely passed when my husband began to show symptoms of a domineering and obstinate spirit. If I requested him to do anything for me, he would surely refuse; if I expressed a wish to go anywhere for recreation, even if it would not cost him a farthing nor occupy more than an hour or two of time, he would certainly remain in bed the greater part of the day; and if I happened to look disappointed or let a murmur escape me, he would rise, kick me, and probably lock me out of the room.

Should he remain much longer from home than I expected, and on his return he should discover the least appearance of anxiety on my countenance, he would meet me with an oath, and pronounce me a fool. When I married him I supposed him in affluent circumstances; but soon the contrary was revealed – he was deeply involved. My fortune was too little to pay his debts; and in his absence I voluntarily endured privations to enable me to clear them off, which I did in six months. This had scarcely been done, when he boldly told me he should expect me to deprive myself of some comforts to which I had been accustomed, and devote the money thus saved to the exigencies of some of his relations. When I remonstrated, he beat me so violently that I bore the marks for some considerable time.

All this I felt the more, perhaps, through being naturally of a most sensitive disposition, and being an only child I was brought up under the care of doting parents. I left home and all I held dear for him. I am now six hundred miles from my native place, without a friend but my husband, and of him I am afraid. He will sometimes express the utmost sorrow for what he has done, and earnestly solicit my forgiveness, which he readily obtains; but, perhaps, before twenty-four hours are elapsed, something new offends him, and the same treatment is repeated. Now, Mr. Editor, can you tell me what I ought to do? I am ashamed to confess to my parents. I cannot ask counsel of my acquaintances, for I should thereby betray my husband. With all his faults I love him dearer than my whole life; and, oh! did he but show me common respect, I could idolise him!

– YOUR CASE is indeed a painful one. Many of the like vicissitudes of marriage might, we think, be averted if the character of each were more deeply studied beforehand. You say your husband has his calmer moments, when he expresses regret for his bad conduct towards you. Choose a favourable opportunity; then firmly but affectionately tell him that, although your love for him has induced you thus long to put up with his ill-treatment, you can no longer bear it, and you must appeal to your friends. This threat alone may exercise a beneficial influence, and may lead him to reflect upon his former brutality.

The vast majority of marriages, of course, did not degenerate into violence, but men had an ingrained idea of a woman's function. Letters from wives complained of their husband's indifference to them. Many men, it appears, gave the impression that the world outside was so much more interesting and absorbing than relationships at home. A typical example came from 'A Wife (Southwark)', though the Beetons' reply can hardly have helped solve the unfortunate woman's problem:

My husband is a strong-minded, clever man, who consequently looks down on those inferior to him in intellect, and has a great contempt for men who take advice from their wives. This hurts my feelings much; for although I would not intrude on his moments of solitude, I know well there are times when advice and sympathy would calm and soften down his irritation, could he divest himself of the foolish notion that it is derogatory to man to take counsel from woman. Does his conduct betoken a want of love? Do tell me how to win my husband's confidence.

–THE COMPLAINT of A Wife is one with which we sympathise deeply; for, from the tenor of her communication we are assured she is really well calculated to be a help-meet to her husband. The feeling shown by him is one which requires most delicate treatment, and we should advise as follows:– Seek your husband in his moments of gloom and, instead of reverting to it, insensibly divert his attention by reading aloud, singing some simple song, or amusing him with the delightful chit-chat in which ladies so much excel. When you have so far made him forget himself, tell him candidly you know there is something on his mind, and your happiness is at stake should he refuse to confide it to you. This, if he love you, will have the desired effect; and a wife's gentle sympathy will meet with its reward.

———

'The little girl who was unkind to her sister'. Victorian literature was full of moral tales, and the nursery was regarded as a training ground for the future.

A WOMAN'S PLACE

In some ways times have changed little – men in Mrs Beeton's day could not resist picking up the magazine, curious to discover what their women were reading about. And, judging by the handful of apopleptic letters, they did not approve of what they saw. One persistent correspondent from Gray's Inn, who signed himself 'Coelebs', probably mirrored the general attitude of many male readers:

> Up to the last two months I have been most happy in the affections of a young lady, whom I have fondly pictured as my wife. I am now most deeply concerned to find that she has taken to authorship, and has gained a prize from you for composition. If there is one thing I have a horror of more than another it is a *blue*. I would rather marry a woman who could not write her name than one that could pen the best essay ever produced. How can such a one be presumed to attend to household matters? Instead of darning stockings, I shall find her writing essays on 'The Rights Of Woman.' Can I expect her to descend from her Pegasus, think you, to make my tea? Altogether my prospect appears very inky, and should I not be justified in affording her, in my own person, a true subject for an essay 'On The Inconsistency Of Man'?

It was a subject close to the Beeton's heart, and Sam lost no time in putting 'Coelebs' firmly in his place:

> COELEBS can never be so prejudiced or narrow-minded as he would lead us to suppose. Are we to infer from what he says that he thinks ignorance qualifies a woman better for the performance of her complicated duties than intelligence? What companionship, what sympathy, what co-operation can a well-educated man, or a man of the world, find in a partner of contracted ideas or confined education; a partner without judgement, without general information and refined tastes?
>
> We pity Coelebs if he imagines darning holes in a stocking, or pouring out a cup of tea cannot be performed by an intelligent woman as well as by an ignorant one. The really well-educated never think any duty beneath them. For our own part, we consider the sympathy and affection of an intellectual woman one of the greatest boons heaven has bestowed on man.

Mrs Beeton shared her husband's sensitivity to such issues but, as a Victorian woman herself, was not over-sympathetic to men in general. She was friendly, sociable and well-loved within her own circle, but had a short fuse which was occasionally noticeable outside. On their return from the Killarney holiday, the Beetons stopped to inspect the much-admired tubular railway bridge over the Menai Straits, one of the newest engineering wonders of the Victorian world. Later, they strolled in the Bangor hills and found themselves suddenly lost. In a line in her diary she testily recounts: 'Two very stupid boys could not tell us the way . . .'

In *Household Management*, between the lines of solid advice, her regard for man periodically surfaces:

> The great object of the grazier is to procure an animal that will yield the greatest pecuniary return in the shortest time. All sheep will not do this alike; some, like men, are so restless and irritable that no system of feeding, however good, will develop their frames, or make them fat.

If men insisted on behaving like sheep, then Mrs Beeton seemed bent on tutoring her readers to raise their husbands like them, too. She had an abiding theme that feeding, and prolonged exposure to the delights of home, would speed their domestication. She pursues it with a singleness of purpose, hammering home the message at every opportunity:

> Musical evenings make additional attractions for home and increase its pleasures. Where music is cultivated by the mistress of a house, or by the daughters, husbands and brothers are generally found 'at home' in the evenings.

In Mrs Beeton's eyes the rehabilitation of the male had been a slow process:

> In former times, when the bottle circulated freely among guests, it was necessary for the ladies to retire earlier than they do at present, for the gentlemen of the company soon became unfit to conduct themselves with that decorum which is essential in the presence of ladies. Thanks, however, to the improvement in modern society . . . temperance is, in these happy days, a striking feature in the character of a gentleman.

THE
SERVANTS' MAGAZINE.

No. 14. NEW SERIES.]   1 FEBRUARY, 1868.   [PRICE ONE PENNY.

Some middle-class children grew up more familiar with nanny than their parents.

Once the husband had been reclaimed from his club, or eating-house in town, it is unclear what was next expected of him. *Household Management* was an indispensable manual for encouraging husbands to spend more time at home, and thus, hopefully, sharing their responsibilities. But the woman who had fought long and hard to get him there was then left to her own devices. Isabella's own married life was so far removed from that of her readers, they might have found it impossible to relate to advice based on her experiences.

An important part of a woman's accepted role was that of bringing up children. *Household Management* was generally regarded as the housewife's bible because of its marvellous recipes and comprehensive advice on organizing the house and servants. Mrs Beeton on babies, however, is an unpublicized revelation. Parents today would possibly be aghast if advised to study Victorian methods of child-care, but Mrs Beeton's commonsense approach has stood the test of time and, in some respects, was quite ahead of it. She took a courageous stand against many of the traditional rules of bringing up babies. Mrs Beeton begs mothers to throw away belly-bindings and all tight clothes for children, preaching that loose, simple garments were far more comfortable. She instructs 'delicate' ladies to develop a taste for large glasses of stout to help their milk flow:

———————————

To the lady accustomed to her Madeira and sherry, this may appear a very vulgar potation for a delicate young mother to take instead of the more subtle and condensed elegance of wine; but as we are writing from experience, and with the vowed object of imparting useful facts and beneficial remedies to our readers, we allow no social distinctions to interfere with our legitimate object . . .

Independently of its invigorating influence on the constitution, porter exerts a marked and specific effect on the secretion of milk, more powerful in exciting an abundant supply of that fluid than any other article within the range of the physician's art; and, in cases of deficient quantity, is the most certain, speedy, and the healthiest means that can be employed to insure a quick and abundant flow . . . The quantity taken must depend upon the natural strength of the mother, the age and demand made by the infant on the parent, and other causes; but the amount should vary from one to two pints a day, never taking less than half a pint at a time.

———————————

SERVANTGALISM.

Mistress. "WHY, NURSE—WHAT A TERRIBLE DISTURBANCE!—PRAY, WHAT IS THE MATTER?"
Nurse (addicted to Pen and Ink). "OH, MUM, IT'S DREADFUL!—HERE'S NEETHER ME NOR MARY CAN'T ANSWER NONE OF OUR
LETTERS FOR THE RACKET!"

She stresses the advantages of open windows and fresh air. And, at a time when the 'healing qualities' of castor oil were universally acknowledged, she refers to the vile concoction as 'that disgusting grease'. As Mrs Beeton calls out for someone to invent nappies without pins, and baby clothes of a 'cool and elastic material', we can assume she would have been delighted at the invention of disposable nappies and the stretch terry-towelling 'Baby-gro' – even if it was almost a century and a half later. If the ingenious Isabella had lived longer, harassed mums might perhaps have had them sooner.

Servants were employed to look after the children, but occasionally needed watching themselves.

THE MANNER in which an infant is encircled in a bandage called the 'roller', as if it had fractured ribs, compressing those organs –

that, living on suction, must be, for the health of the child, to a certain degree distended to obtain sufficient aliment from the fluid imbibed – is perfectly preposterous. Our humanity, as well as our duty, calls upon us at once to abrogate and discountenance by every means in our power. Instead of the process of washing and dressing being made, as with the adult, a refreshment and comfort, it is by the dawdling manner in which it is performed, the multiplicity of things used, and the perpetual change of position of the infant to adjust its complicated clothing, rendered an operation of positive irritation and anoyance. We, therefore, entreat all mothers to regard this subject in its true light, and study to the utmost simplicity in dress, and dispatch in the process.

. . . For the moment setting health and comfort out of the question, we beg mothers to simplify their baby's dress as much as possible; and not only to put on as little as is absolutely necessary, but to make that as simple in its contrivance and adjustment as it will admit of; to avoid belly-bands, rollers, girths and everything that can impede or confine the natural expansion of the digestive organs, on the due performance of whose functions the child lives, thrives, and develops its physical being.

Part of the mistress's daily round was to see how the midday meal in the nursery was progressing.

Tea-time in the nursery – small children rarely ate at the family table with their parents.

It was a testimony of Sam and Isabella's strength and love that, after losing two of their own children, they managed to grow closer, pick up the threads of their life together, and advise others how to avoid similar crises. Notes on infant illnesses make up a considerable proportion of the section on child care.

Isabella's mother's marriage to the rather snobbish Henry Dorling had drawn her into a hectic social life, leaving her eldest daughter with the day-to-day care of the children. Isabella, with the help of her maternal grandmother, Granny Jerram, was often in sole command of them at the Grandstand. Along the way she acquired a vast amount of experience and first-hand knowledge of babies and young children.

It is hardly surprising that, even in her early twenties, she wrote so authoritatively. Much of her work was guided by sound research, sharp intelligence and a lasting respect for Florence Nightingale's *Notes on Nursing*. Isabella frequently praised her methods and her strict attention to hygiene.

Choosing the right calibre of nurse-maid, or nanny, was important for the peace of mind of her middle-class mothers. 'A monthly nurse,' she advised, 'should be between thirty and fifty years of age, sufficiently old to have had a little experience, and yet not too old or infirm to be able to perform various duties requiring strength and bodily vigour . . . Good temper, united to a kind and gentle disposition, is indispensable.' Her general advice is written with a care and understanding not always familiar in the spartan environment of the Victorian nursery:

There is a considerable art in carrying an infant comfortably for itself and for the nursemaid. If she carry it always seated upright on her arm, and presses it too closely against her chest, the stomach of the child is apt to get compressed, and the back fatigued. For her own comfort, a good nurse will frequently vary this position, by changing from one arm to the other, and sometimes by laying across both, raising the head a little. When teaching it to walk, and guiding it by the hand, she should change the hand from time to time, so as to avoid raising one shoulder higher than the other. This is the only way in which a child should be taught to walk; leading-strings and other foolish inventions, which force an infant to make efforts with its shoulders and head forward, before it knows how to use its limbs, will only render it feeble, and retard its progress.

Most children have some bad habit, of which they must be broken; but this is never accomplished by harshness without developing worse evils: kindness, perseverance, and patience in the nurse, are here of the utmost importance. When finger-sucking is one of these habits, the fingers are sometimes rubbed with bitter aloes, or some equally disagreeable substance. Others have dirty habits which are only to be changed by patience, perseverance and, above all, by regularity in the nurse. She should never be permitted to inflict punishment on these occasions, or indeed, on any occasion.

But, if punishment is to be avoided, it is still more necessary that all kinds of indulgences and flattery be equally forbidden. Yielding to the whims of a child – picking up its toys when thrown away in mere wantonness – would be intolerable. A child should never be led to think others inferior to it, to beat a dog, or even the stone against which it falls, as some children are taught to do by silly nurses. Neither should the nurse affect or show alarm at any of the little accidents which must inevitably happen: if it falls, treat it as a trifle; otherwise she encourages a spirit of cowardice and timidity. But she will take care that such accidents are not of frequent occurrence, or the result of neglect.

The nurse should keep the child as clean as possible, and particularly she should train it to habits of cleanliness, so that it should feel uncomfortable when otherwise; watching, especially, that it does not soil itself in eating . . .

Nursemaids would do well to repeat to the parents faithfully and truly the defects they observe in the dispositions of very young children. If properly checked in time, evil propensities may be eradicated; but this should no extend to anything but serious defects; otherwise the intuitive perceptions

Perambulation was often the only time a hard-worked children's maid had to make friends.

which all children possess will construe the act into 'spying' and 'informing', which should never be resorted to in the case of

———————

Mrs Beeton was a singular and remarkable woman, praised in her lifetime and later forgotten and ignored when a pride in light pastry and the skills at presiding with sparkle over a sumptuous dinner spread were no longer considered prerequisites for womanhood. Yet, in her lively, progressive way, she helped many women to overcome the loneliness of marriage and gave the family the importance it deserved. In the climate of her time she was brave, strong-minded and a tireless champion of her sisters everywhere.

On her centenary the *New Statesman* said: 'Mrs Beeton must be judged by the standards, not of Utopia, but of her own age and ours . . . Like other great teachers she is revered, and her advice is ignored. She is, judged by results, the greatest failure of the nineteenth century. May the celebration of her centenary bring about a change of heart . . .' The same, I am sure, could be said another half-century later.

8
Recipes
Classic Beeton Dishes to Re-Create in Your Kitchen

STOCKS FOR ALL KINDS OF SOUPS

RICH STRONG STOCK.

104. INGREDIENTS.—4 lbs. of shin of beef, 4 lbs. of knuckle of veal, ¾ lb. of good lean ham; any poultry trimmings; 3 small onions, 3 small carrots, 3 turnips (the latter should be omitted in summer, lest they ferment), 1 head of celery, a few chopped mushrooms, when obtainable; 1 tomato, a bunch of savoury herbs, not forgetting parsley; 1½ oz. of salt, 12 white peppercorns, 6 cloves, 3 small blades of mace, 4 quarts of water.

Mode.—Line a delicately clean stewpan with the ham cut in thin broad slices, carefully trimming off all its rusty fat; cut up the beef and veal in pieces about 3 inches square, and lay them on the ham; set it on the stove, and draw it down, and stir frequently. When the meat is equally browned, put in the beef and veal bones, the poultry trimmings, and pour in the cold water. Skim well, and occasionally add a little cold water, to stop its boiling, until it becomes quite clear; then put in all the other ingredients, and simmer very slowly for 5 hours. Do not let it come to a brisk boil, that the stock be not wasted, and that its colour may be preserved. Strain through a very fine hair sieve, or tammy, and it will be fit for use.

Time.—5 hours. *Average cost,* 1s. 3d. per quart.

MEDIUM STOCK.

105. INGREDIENTS.—4 lbs. of shin of beef, or 4 lbs. of knuckle of veal, or 2 lbs. of each; any bones, trimmings of poultry, or fresh meat, ½ a lb. of lean bacon or ham, 2 oz. of butter, 2 large onions, each stuck with 3 cloves; 1 turnip, 3 carrots, ½ a leek, 1 head of celery, 2 oz. of salt, ½ a teaspoonful of whole pepper, 1 large blade of mace, 1 small bunch of savoury herbs, 4 quarts and ½ pint of cold water.

Mode.—Cut up the meat and bacon or ham into pieces about 3 inches square; rub the butter on the bottom of the stewpan; put in ½ a pint of water, the meat, and all the other ingredients. Cover the stewpan, and place it on a sharp fire, occasionally stirring its contents. When the bottom of the pan becomes covered with a pale, jelly-like substance, add 4 quarts of cold water, and simmer very gently for 5 hours. As

we have said before, do not let it boil quickly. Skim off every particle of grease whilst it is doing, and strain it through a fine hair sieve.

This is the basis of many of the soups afterwards mentioned, and will be found quite strong enough for ordinary purposes.

Time.—5½ hours. *Average cost,* 9d. per quart.

ECONOMICAL STOCK.

106. INGREDIENTS.—The liquor in which a joint of meat has been boiled, say 4 quarts; trimmings of fresh meat or poultry, shank-bones, &c., roast-beef bones, any pieces the larder may furnish; vegetables, spices, and the same seasoning as in the foregoing recipe.

Mode.—Let all the ingredients simmer gently for 6 hours, taking care to skim carefully at first. Strain it off, and put by for use.

Time.—6 hours. *Average cost,* 3d. per quart.

FISH STOCK.

192. INGREDIENTS.—2 lbs. of beef or veal (these can be omitted), any kind of white fish trimmings, of fish which are to be dressed for table, 2 onions, the rind of ½ a lemon, a bunch of sweet herbs, 2 carrots, 2 quarts of water.

Mode.—Cut up the fish, and put it, with the other ingredients, into the water. Simmer for 2 hours; skim the liquor carefully, and strain it. When a richer stock is wanted, fry the vegetables and fish before adding the water.

Time.—2 hours. *Average cost,* with meat, 10d. per quart; without, 3d.

Note.—Do not make fish stock long before it is wanted, as it soon turns sour.

WHITE STOCK.
(*To be Used in the Preparation of White Soups.*)

107. INGREDIENTS.—4 lbs. of knuckle of veal, any poultry trimmings, 4 slices of lean ham, 1 carrot, 2 onions, 1 head of celery,

---
117

12 white peppercorns, 1 oz. of salt, 1 blade of mace, 1 oz. butter, 4 quarts of water.

Mode.—Cut up the veal, and put it with the bones and trimmings of poultry, and the ham, into the stewpan, which has been rubbed with the butter. Moisten with ½ a pint of water, and simmer till the gravy begins to flow. Then add the 4 quarts of water and the remainder of the ingredients; simmer for 5 hours. After skimming and straining it carefully through a very fine hair sieve, it will be ready for use.

Time.—5½ hours. *Average cost*, 9d. per quart.

Note.—When stronger stock is desired, double the quantity of veal, or put

iu an old fowl. The liquor in which a young turkey has been boiled, is an excellent addition to all white stock or soups.

Note.—It is on a good stock, or first good broth and sauce, that excellence in cookery depends. If the preparation of this basis of the culinary art is intrusted to negligent or ignorant persons, and the stock is not well skimmed, but indifferent results will be obtained. The stock will never be clear; and when it is obliged to be clarified, it is deteriorated both in quality and flavour. In the proper management of the stock-pot an immense deal of trouble is saved, inasmuch as one stock, in a small dinner, serves for all purposes. Above all things, the greatest economy, consistent with excellence, should be practised, and the price of everything which enters the kitchen correctly ascertained. The *theory* of this part of Household Management may appear trifling; but its practice is extensive, and therefore it requires the best attention.

SOUPS

SOUP A LA CANTATRICE.

(An Excellent Soup, very Beneficial for the Voice.)

119. INGREDIENTS.—3 oz. of sago, ⅓ pint of cream, the yolks of 3 eggs, 1 lump of sugar, and seasoning to taste, 1 bay-leaf (if liked), 2 quarts of medium stock No. 105.

Mode.—Having washed the sago in boiling water, let it be gradually added to the nearly boiling stock. Simmer for ¼ an hour, when it should be well dissolved. Beat up the yolks of the eggs, add to them the boiling cream; stir these quickly in the soup, and serve immediately. Do not let the soup boil, or the eggs will curdle.

Time.—40 minutes. *Average cost*, 1s. 6d. per quart.

Seasonable all the year.

Sufficient for 8 persons.

Note.—This is a soup, the principal ingredients of which, sago and eggs, have always been deemed very beneficial to the chest and throat. In various quantities, and in different preparations, these have been partaken of by the principal singers of the day, including the celebrated Swedish Nightingale, Jenny Lind, and, as they have always avowed, with considerable advantage to the voice, in singing.

CUCUMBER SOUP (French Recipe).

127. INGREDIENTS.—1 large cucumber, a piece of butter the size of a walnut, a little chervil and sorrel cut in large pieces salt and pepper to taste, the yolks of 2 eggs, 1 gill of cream, 1 quart of medium stock No. 105.

Mode.—Pare the cucumber, quarter it, and take out the seeds; cut it in thin slices, put these on a plate with a little salt, to draw the water from them; drain, and put them in your stewpan, with the butter. When they are warmed through, without being browned, pour the stock on them. Add the sorrel, chervil, and seasoning, and boil for 40 minutes. Mix the well-beaten yolks of the eggs with the cream, which add at the moment of serving.

Time.—1 hour. *Average cost*, 1s. 2d. per quart.

Seasonable from June to September.

Sufficient for 4 persons.

THE CUCUMBER.—The antiquity of this fruit is very great. In the sacred writings we find that the people of Israel regretted it, whilst sojourning in the desert; and at the present time, the cucumber, and other fruits of its class, form a large portion of the food of the Egyptian people. By the Eastern nations generally, as well as by the Greeks and Romans, it was greatly esteemed. Like the melon, it was originally brought from Asia by the Romans, and in the 14th century it was common in England, although, in the time of the wars of "the Roses," it seems no longer to have been cultivated. It is a cold food, and of difficult digestion when eaten raw. As a preserved sweetmeat, however, it is esteemed one of the most agreeable.

SOUP MAIGRE (i.e. without Meat).

136. INGREDIENTS.—6 oz. butter, 6 onions sliced, 4 heads of celery, 2 lettuces, a small bunch of parsley, 2 handfuls of spinach, 3 pieces of bread-crust, 2 blades of mace, salt and pepper to taste, the yolks of 2 eggs, 3 teaspoonfuls of vinegar, 2 quarts of water.

Mode.—Melt the butter in a stewpan, and put in the onions to stew gently for 3 or 4 minutes; then add the celery, spinach, lettuces, and parsley, cut small. Stir the ingredients well for 10 minutes. Now put in the water, bread, seasoning, and mace. Boil gently for 1½ hour, and, at the moment of serving, beat in the yolks of the eggs and the vinegar, but do not let it boil, or the eggs will curdle.

Time.—2 hours. *Average cost*, 6d. per quart.

Seasonable all the year.

Sufficient for 8 persons.

THE LETTUCE.—This is one of the acetarious vegetables, which comprise a large class, chiefly used as pickles, salads, and other condiments. The lettuce has in all antiquity been distinguished as a kitchen-garden plant. It was, without preparation, eaten by the Hebrews with the Paschal lamb; the Greeks delighted in it, and the Romans, in the time of Domitian, had it prepared with eggs, and served in the first course at their tables, merely to excite their appetites. Its botanical name is *Lactuca*, so called from the milky juice it exudes when its stalks are cut. It possesses a narcotic virtue, noticed by ancient physicians; and even in our day a lettuce supper is deemed conducive to repose. Its proper character, however, is that of a cooling summer vegetable, not very nutritive, but serving as a corrective, or diluent of animal food.

LETTUCE.

SOUP A LA SOLFERINO (Sardinian Recipe).

154. INGREDIENTS.—4 eggs, ½ pint of cream, 2 oz. of fresh butter, salt and pepper to taste, a little flour to thicken, 2 quarts of bouillon, No. 105.

Mode.—Beat the eggs, put them into a stewpan, and add the cream, butter, and seasoning; stir in as much flour as will bring it to the consistency of dough; make it into balls, either round or egg-shaped, and fry them in butter; put them in the tureen, and pour the boiling bouillon over them.

Time.—1 hour. *Average cost*, 1s. 3d. per quart.

Seasonable all the year.

Sufficient for 8 persons.

Note.—This receipe was communicated to the Editress by an English gentleman, who was present at the battle of Solferino, on June 24, 1859, and who was requested by some of Victor Emmanuel's troops, on the day before the battle, to partake of a portion of their *potage*. He willingly enough consented, and found that these clever campaigners had made a most palatable dish from very easily-procured materials. In sending the recipe for insertion in this work, he has, however, Anglicised, and somewhat, he thinks, improved it.

OYSTER SOUP.

196. INGREDIENTS.—6 dozen of oysters, 2 quarts of white stock, ½ pint of cream, 2 oz. of butter, 1½ oz. of flour; salt, cayenne, and mace to taste.

Mode.—Scald the oysters in their own liquor; take them out, beard them, and put them in a tureen. Take a pint of the stock, put in the beards and the liquor, which must be carefully strained, and simmer for ½ an hour. Take it off the fire, strain it again, and add the remainder of the stock with the seasoning and mace. Bring it to a boil, add the thickening of butter and flour, simmer for 5 minutes, stir in the boiling cream, pour it over the oysters, and serve.

Time.—1 hour. *Average cost*, 2s. 8d. per quart.

Seasonable from September to April.

Sufficient for 8 persons.

Note.—This soup can be made less rich by using milk instead of cream, and thickening with arrowroot instead of butter and flour.

REGENCY SOUP.

182. INGREDIENTS.—Any bones and remains of any cold game, such as of pheasants, partridges, &c.; 2 carrots, 2 small onions, 1 head of celery, 1 turnip, ¼ lb. of pearl barley, the yolks of 3 eggs boiled hard, ¼ pint of cream, salt to taste, 2 quarts of stock No. 105, or common stock, No. 106.

Mode.—Place the bones or remains of game in the stewpan, with the vegetables sliced; pour over the stock, and simmer for 2 hours; skim off all the fat, and strain it. Wash the barley, and boil it in 2 or 3 waters before putting it to the soup; finish simmering in the soup, and when the barley is done, take out half, and pound the other half with the yolks of the eggs. When you have finished pounding, rub it through a clean tammy, add the cream, and salt if necessary; give one boil, and serve very hot, putting in the barley that was taken out first.

Time.—2½ hours. *Average cost*, 1s. per quart, if made with medium stock, or 6d. per quart, with common stock.

Seasonable from September to March.

Sufficient for 8 persons.

FISH

BAKED SOLES.

320. INGREDIENTS.—2 soles, ¼ lb. of butter, egg, and bread crumbs, minced parsley, 1 glass of sherry, lemon-juice; cayenne and salt to taste.

Mode. — Clean, skin, and well wash the fish, and dry them thoroughly in a cloth. Brush them over with egg, sprinkle with bread crumbs mixed with a little minced parsley, lay them in a large flat baking-dish, white side uppermost; or if it will not hold the two soles, they may each be laid on a dish by itself; but they must not be put one on the top of the other. Melt the butter, and pour it over the whole, and bake for 20 minutes. Take a portion of the gravy that flows from the fish, add the wine, lemon-juice, and seasoning, give it one boil, skim, pour it *under* the fish, and serve.

Time.—20 minutes. *Average cost*, 1s. to 2s. per pair.

Seasonable at any time.

Sufficient for 4 or 5 persons.

TO CHOOSE SOLES.—This fish should be both thick and firm. If the skin is difficult to be taken off, and the flesh looks grey, it is good.

THE SOLE.

THE SOLE.—This ranks next to the turbot in point of excellence among our flat fish. It is abundant on the British coasts, but those of the western shores are much superior in size to those taken on the northern. The finest are caught in Torbay, and frequently weigh 8 or 10 lbs. per pair. Its flesh being firm, white, and delicate, is greatly esteemed.

LOBSTER PATTIES (an Entree).

277. INGREDIENTS.—Minced lobster, 4 tablespoonfuls of béchamel, 6 drops of anchovy sauce, lemon-juice, cayenne to taste.

Mode.—Line the patty-pans with puff-paste, and put into each a small piece of bread: cover with paste, brush over with egg, and bake of a light colour. Take as much lobster as is required, mince the meat very fine, and add the above ingredients; stir it over the fire for 5 minutes; remove the lids of the patty-cases, take out the bread, fill with the mixture, and replace the covers.

Seasonable at any time.

LOCAL ATTACHMENT OF THE LOBSTER.—It is said that the attachment of this animal is strong to some particular parts of the sea, a circumstance celebrated in the following lines:—

> " Nought like their home the constant lobsters prize,
> And foreign shores and seas unknown despise.
> Though cruel hands the banish'd wretch expel,
> And force the captive from his native cell,
> He will, if freed, return with anxious care,
> Find the known rock, and to his home repair;
> No novel customs learns in different seas,
> But wonted food and home-taught manners please."

POTTED LOBSTER.

278. INGREDIENTS.—2 lobsters; seasoning to taste, of nutmeg, pounded mace, white pepper, and salt; ¼ lb. of butter, 3 or 4 bay-leaves.

Mode.—Take out the meat carefully from the shell, but do not cut it up. Put some butter at the bottom of a dish, lay in the lobster as evenly as possible, with the bay-leaves and seasoning between. Cover with butter, and bake for ¾ hour in a gentle oven. When done, drain the whole on a sieve, and lay the pieces in potting-jars, with the seasoning about them. When cold, pour over it clarified butter, and, if very highly seasoned, it will keep some time.

Time.—¾ hour. *Average cost* for this quantity, 4s. 4d.

Seasonable at any time.

Note.—Potted lobster may be used cold, or as a *fricassee* with cream sauce.

HOW THE LOBSTER FEEDS.—The pincers of the lobster's large claws are furnished with nobs, and those of the other, are always serrated. With the former, it keeps firm hold of the stalks of submarine plants, and with the latter, it cuts and minces its food with great dexterity. The knobbed, or numb claw, as it is called by fishermen, is sometimes on the right and sometimes on the left, indifferently.

OYSTER PATTIES (an Entree).

289. INGREDIENTS.—2 dozen oysters, 2 oz. butter, 3 tablespoonfuls of cream, a little lemon-juice, 1 blade of pounded mace; cayenne to taste.

Mode.—Scald the oysters in their own liquor, beard them, and cut each one into 3 pieces. Put the butter into a stewpan, dredge in sufficient flour to dry it up; add the strained oyster-liquor with the other ingredients; put in the oysters, and let them heat gradually, but not boil fast. Make the patty-cases as directed for lobster patties, No. 277: fill with the oyster mixture, and replace the covers.

Time.—2 minutes for the oysters to simmer in the mixture.

Average cost, exclusive of the patty-cases, 1*s*. 4*d*.

Seasonable from September to April.

The Oyster Fishery.—The oyster fishery in Britain is esteemed of so much importance, that it is regulated by a Court of Admiralty. In the month of May, the fishermen are allowed to take the oysters, in order to separate the spawn from the cultch, the latter of which is thrown in again, to preserve the bed for the future. After this month, it is felony to carry away the cultch, and otherwise punishable to take any oyster, between the shells of which, when closed, a shilling will rattle.

TO KEEP OYSTERS.

290. Put them in a tub, and cover them with salt and water. Let them remain for 12 hours, when they are to be taken out, and allowed to stand for another 12 hours without water. If left without water every alternate 12 hours, they will be much better than if constantly kept in it. Never put the same water twice to them.

OYSTERS FRIED IN BATTER.

291. Ingredients.—½ pint of oysters, 2 eggs, ½ pint of milk, sufficient flour to make the batter; pepper and salt to taste; when liked, a little nutmeg; hot lard.

Mode.—Scald the oysters in their own liquor, beard them, and lay them on a cloth, to drain thoroughly. Break the eggs into a basin, mix the flour with them, add the milk gradually, with nutmeg and seasoning, and put the oysters in the batter. Make some lard hot in a deep frying-pan, put in the oysters, one at a time; when done, take them up with a sharp-pointed skewer, and dish them on a napkin. Fried oysters are frequently used for garnishing boiled fish, and then a few bread crumbs should be added to the flour.

Time.—5 or 6 minutes. *Average cost* for this quantity, 1*s*. 10*d*.

Seasonable from September to April.

Sufficient for 3 persons.

COD PIE.

(*Economical.*)

I.

235. Ingredients.—Any remains of cold cod, 12 oysters, sufficient melted butter to moisten it; mashed potatoes enough to fill up the dish.

Mode.—Flake the fish from the bone, and carefully take away all the skin. Lay it in a pie-dish, pour over the melted butter and oysters (or oyster sauce, if there is any left), and cover with mashed potatoes. Bake for ½ an hour, and send to table of a nice brown colour.

Time.— ½ hour.

Seasonable from November to March.

II.

236. Ingredients.—2 slices of cod; pepper and salt to taste; ⅛ a teaspoonful of grated nutmeg, 1 large blade of pounded mace, 2 oz. of butter, ½ pint of stock No. 107, a paste crust (*see* Pastry). For sauce, 1 tablespoonful of stock, ¼ pint of cream or milk, thickening of flour or butter; lemon-peel chopped very fine to taste; 12 oysters.

Mode.—Lay the cod in salt for 4 hours, then wash it and place it in a dish; season, and add the butter and stock; cover with the crust, and bake for 1 hour, or rather more. Now make the sauce, by mixing the ingredients named above; give it one boil, and pour it into the pie by a hole made at the top of the crust, which can easily be covered by a small piece of pastry cut and baked in any fanciful shape—such as a leaf, or otherwise.

Time.—1½ hour. *Average cost*, with fresh fish, 2*s*. 6*d*.

Seasonable from November to March.

Sufficient for 6 persons.

Note.—The remains of cold fish may be used for this pie.

Preserving Cod.—Immediately as the cod are caught, their heads are cut off. They are then opened, cleaned, and salted, when they are stowed away in the hold of the vessel, in beds of five or six yards square, head to tail, with a layer of salt to each layer of fish. When they have lain in this state three or four days, in order that the water may drain from them, they are shifted into a different part of the vessel, and again salted. Here they remain till the vessel is loaded, when they are sometimes cut into thick pieces and packed in barrels for the greater convenience of carriage.

BOILED SALMON.

301. Ingredients.—6 oz. of salt to each gallon of water,—sufficient water to cover the fish.

Mode.—Scale and clean the fish, and be particular that no blood is left inside; lay it in the fish-kettle with sufficient cold water to cover it, adding salt in the above proportion. Bring it quickly to a boil, take off all the scum, and let it simmer gently till the fish is done, which will be when the meat separates easily from the bone. Experience alone can teach the cook to fix the time for boiling fish; but it is especially to be remembered, that it should never be underdressed, as then nothing is more unwholesome. Neither let it remain in the kettle after it is sufficiently cooked, as that would render it insipid, watery, and colourless. Drain it, and if not wanted for a few minutes, keep it warm by means of warm cloths laid over it. Serve on a hot napkin, garnish with cut lemon and parsley, and send lobster or shrimp sauce, and plain melted butter to table with it. A dish of dressed cucumber usually accompanies this fish.

Time.—8 minutes to each lb. for large thick salmon; 6 minutes for thin fish. *Average cost*, in full season, 1*s*. 3*d*. per lb.

Seasonable from April to August.

Sufficient, ½ lb., or rather less, for each person.

CRIMPED SALMON.

304. Salmon is frequently dressed in this way at many fashionable tables, but must be very fresh, and cut into slices 2 or 3 inches thick. Lay these in cold salt and water for 1 hour; have ready some boiling water, salted, as in recipe No. 301, and well skimmed; put in the fish, and simmer gently for ¼ hour, or rather more; should it be very thick, garnish the same as boiled salmon, and serve with the same sauces.

Time.—¼ hour, more or less, according to size.

Note.—Never use vinegar with salmon, as it spoils the taste and colour of the fish.

THE SALMON.

The Salmon Tribe.—This is the Abdominal fish, forming the fourth of the orders of Linnæus. They are distinguished from other fishes by having two dorsal fins, of which the hindmost is fleshy and without rays. They have teeth both on the tongue and in the jaws, whilst the body is covered with round and minutely striated scales.

SALMON A LA GENEVESE.

307. INGREDIENTS.—2 slices of salmon, 2 chopped shalots, a little parsley, a small bunch of herbs, 2 bay-leaves, 2 carrots, pounded mace, pepper and salt to taste, 4 tablespoonfuls of Madeira, ½ pint of white stock (No. 107), thickening of butter and flour, 1 teaspoonful of essence of anchovies, the juice of 1 lemon, cayenne and salt to taste.

Mode.—Rub the bottom of a stewpan over with butter, and put in the shalots, herbs, bay-leaves, carrots, mace, and seasoning; stir them for 10 minutes over a clear fire, and add the Madeira or sherry; simmer gently for ½ hour, and strain through a sieve over the fish, which stew in this gravy. As soon as the fish is sufficiently cooked, take away all the liquor, except a little to keep the salmon moist, and put it into another stewpan; add the stock, thicken with butter and flour, and put in the anchovies, lemon-juice, cayenne, and salt; lay the salmon on a hot dish, pour over it part of the sauce, and serve the remainder in a tureen.

Time.—1½ hour. *Average cost* for this quantity, 3*s.* 6*d.*

Sufficient for 4 or 5 persons.

SAUCES, PICKLES

355. THE PREPARATION AND APPEARANCE OF SAUCES AND GRAVIES are of the highest consequence, and in nothing does the talent and taste of the cook more display itself. Their special adaptability to the various viands they are to accompany cannot be too much studied, in order that they may harmonize and blend with them as perfectly, so to speak, as does a pianoforto accompaniment with the voice of the singer.

358. SAUCES SHOULD POSSESS A DECIDED CHARACTER; and whether sharp or sweet, savoury or plain, they should carry out their names in a distinct manner, although, of course, not so much flavoured as to make them too piquant on the one hand, or too mawkish on the other.

359. GRAVIES AND SAUCES SHOULD BE SENT TO TABLE VERY HOT; and there is all the more necessity for the cook to see to this point, as, from their being usually served in small quantities, they are more liable to cool quickly than if they were in a larger body. Those sauces, of which cream or eggs form a component part, should be well stirred, as soon as these ingredients are added to them, and must never be allowed to boil; as, in that case, they would instantly curdle.

ANCHOVY SAUCE FOR FISH.

362. INGREDIENTS.—4 anchovies, 1 oz. of butter, ½ pint of melted butter, cayenne to taste.

Mode.—Bone the anchovies, and pound them in a mortar to a paste, with 1 oz. of butter. Make the melted butter hot, stir in the pounded anchovies and cayenne; simmer for 3 or 4 minutes; and if liked, add a squeeze of lemon-juice. A more general and expeditious way of making this sauce is to stir in 1½ tablespoonfuls of anchovy essence to ½ pint of melted butter, and to add seasoning to taste. Boil the whole up for 1 minute, and serve hot.

Time.—5 minutes. *Average cost*, 5*d.* for ½ pint.

Sufficient, this quantity, for a brill, small turbot, 3 or 4 soles, &c.

CAYENNE.—This is the most acrid and stimulating spice with which we are acquainted. It is a powder prepared from several varieties of the capsicum annual East-India plants, of which there are three so far naturalized in this country as to be able to grow in the open air: these are the Guinea, the Cherry, and the Bell pepper. All the pods of these are extremely pungent to the taste, and in the green state are used by us as a pickle. When ripe, they are ground into cayenne pepper, and sold as a condiment. The best of this, however, is made in the West Indies, from what is called the *Bird* pepper, on account of hens and turkeys being extremely partial to it. It is imported ready for use. Of the capsicum species of plants there are five; but the principal are,—1. *Capsicum annuum*, the common long-podded capsicum, which is cultivated in our gardens, and of which there are two varieties, one with red, and another with yellow fruit. 2. *Capsicum baccatum*, or bird pepper, which rises with a shrubby stalk four or five feet high, with its berries growing at the division of the branches: this is small, oval-shaped, and of a bright-red colour, from which, as we have said, the best cayenne is made. 3. *Capsicum grossum*, the bell-pepper: the fruit of this is red, and is the only kind fit for pickling.

THE CAPSICUM.

ASPARAGUS SAUCE.

365. INGREDIENTS.—1 bunch of green asparagus, salt, 1 oz. of fresh butter, 1 small bunch of parsley, 3 or 4 green onions, 1 large lump of sugar, 4 tablespoonfuls of sauce tournée.

Mode.—Break the asparagus in the tender part, wash well, and put them into boiling salt and water to render them green. When they are tender, take them out, and put them into cold water; drain them on a cloth till all moisture is absorbed from them. Put the butter in a stewpan, with the parsley and onions; lay in the asparagus, and fry the whole over a sharp fire for 5 minutes. Add salt, the sugar and sauce tournée, and simmer for another 5 minutes. Rub all through a tammy, and if not a very good colour, use a little spinach green. This sauce should be rather sweet.

Time.—Altogether 40 minutes.

Average cost for this quantity, 1*s.* 4*d.*

BENGAL RECIPE FOR MAKING MANGO CHETNEY.

392. INGREDIENTS.—1½ lbs. of moist sugar, ¾ lb. of salt, ¼ lb. of garlic, ¼ lb. of onions, ¾ lb. of powdered ginger, ¼ lb. of dried chilies, ¾ lb. of mustard-seed, ¾ lb. of stoned raisins, 2 bottles of best vinegar, 30 large unripe sour apples.

Mode.—The sugar must be made into syrup; the garlic, onions, and ginger be finely pounded in a mortar; the mustard-seed be washed in cold vinegar, and dried in the sun; the apples be peeled, cored, and sliced, and boiled in a bottle and a half of the vinegar. When all this is done, and the apples are quite cold, put them into a large pan, and gradually mix the whole of the rest of the ingredients, including the remaining half-bottle of vinegar. It must be well stirred until the whole is thoroughly blended, and then put into bottles for use. Tie a piece of wet bladder over the mouths of the bottles, after they are well corked. This chetney is very superior to any which can be bought, and one trial will prove it to be delicious.

Note.—This recipe was given by a native to an English lady, who had long been a resident in India, and who, since her return to her native country, has become quite celebrated amongst her friends for the excellence of this Eastern relish.

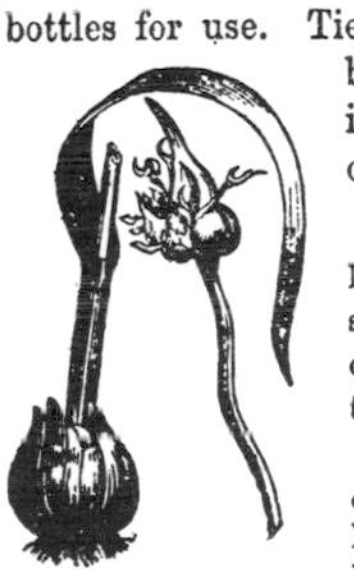

GARLIC.

GARLIC.—The smell of this plant is generally considered offensive, and it is the most acrimonious in its taste of the whole of the alliaceous tribe. In 1548 it was introduced to England from the shores of the Mediterranean, where it is abundant, and in Sicily it grows naturally. It was in greater repute with our ancestors than it is with ourselves, although it is still used as a seasoning herb. On the continent, especially in Italy, it is much used, and the French consider it an essential in many made dishes.

BÉCHAMEL, or FRENCH WHITE SAUCE.

367. INGREDIENTS.—1 small bunch of parsley, 2 cloves, ½ bay-leaf, 1 small faggot of savoury herbs, salt to taste; 3 or 4 mushrooms, when obtainable; 2 pints of white stock, 1 pint of cream, 1 tablespoonful of arrowroot.

Mode.—Put the stock into a stewpan, with the parsley, cloves, bay-leaf, herbs, and mushrooms; add a seasoning of salt, but no pepper, as that would give the sauce a dusty appearance, and should be avoided. When it has boiled long enough to extract the flavour of the herbs, &c., strain it, and boil it up quickly again, until it is nearly half-reduced. Now mix the arrowroot smoothly with the cream, and let it simmer very gently for 5 minutes over a slow fire; pour to it the reduced stock, and continue to simmer slowly for 10 minutes, if the sauce be thick. If, on the contrary, it be too thin, it must be stirred over a sharp fire till it thickens. This is the foundation of many kinds of sauces, especially white sauces. Always make it thick, as you can easily thin it with cream, milk, or white stock.

Time.—Altogether, 2 hours. *Average cost,* 1s. per pint.

THE CLOVE.—The clove-tree is a native of the Molucca Islands, particularly Amboyna, and attains the height of a laurel-tree, and no verdure is ever seen under it. From the extremities of the branches quantities of flowers grow, first white; then they become green, and next red and hard, when they have arrived at their clove state. When they become dry, they assume a yellowish hue, which subsequently changes into a dark brown. As an aromatic, the clove is highly stimulating, and yields an abundance of oil. There are several varieties of the clove; the best is called the *royal clove,* which is scarce, and which is blacker and smaller than the other kinds. It is a curious fact, that the flowers, when fully developed, are quite inodorous, and that the real fruit is not in the least aromatic. The form is that of a nail, having a globular head, formed of the four petals of the corolla, and four leaves of the calyx not expanded, with a nearly cylindrical germen, scarcely an inch in length, situate below.

THE CLOVE.

BÉCHAMEL MAIGRE, or WITHOUT MEAT.

368. INGREDIENTS.—2 onions, 1 blade of mace, mushroom trimmings, a small bunch of parsley, 1 oz. of butter, flour, ¼ pint of water, 1 pint of milk, salt, the juice of ½ lemon, 2 eggs.

Mode.—Put in a stewpan the milk, and ½ pint of water, with the onions, mace, mushrooms, parsley, and salt. Let these simmer gently for 20 minutes. In the mean time, rub on a plate 1 oz. of flour and butter; put it to the liquor, and stir it well till it boils up; then place it by the side of the fire, and continue stirring until it is perfectly smooth. Now strain it through a sieve into a basin, after which put it back in the stewpan, and add the lemon-juice. Beat up the yolks of the eggs with about 4 dessertspoonfuls of milk; strain this to the sauce, keep stirring it over the fire, but do not let it boil, lest it curdle.

Time.—Altogether, ¾ hour. *Average cost,* 5d. per pint.

This is a good sauce to pour over boiled fowls when they are a bad colour.

GREEN DUTCH SAUCE, or HOLLANDAISE VERTE.

406. INGREDIENTS.—6 tablespoonfuls of Béchamel, No. 367, seasoning to taste of salt and cayenne, a little parsley-green to colour, the juice of ⅓ a lemon.

Mode.—Put the Béchamel into a saucepan with the seasoning, and bring it to a boil. Make a green colouring by pounding some parsley in a mortar, and squeezing all the juice from it. Let this just simmer, when add it to the sauce. A moment before serving, put in the lemon-juice, but not before; for otherwise the sauce would turn yellow, and its appearance be thus spoiled.

Average cost, 4d.

MEAT

BEEF-STEAK AND KIDNEY PUDDING.

605. INGREDIENTS.—2 lbs. of rump-steak, 2 kidneys, seasoning to taste of salt and black pepper, suet crust made with milk (*see* Pastry), in the proportion of 6 oz. of suet to each 1 lb. of flour.

Mode.—Procure some tender rump steak (that which has been hung a little time), and divide it into pieces about an inch square, and cut each kidney into 8 pieces. Line the dish (of which we have given an engraving) with crust made with suet and flour in the above proportion, leaving a small piece of crust to overlap the edge. Then cover the bottom with a portion of the steak and a few pieces of kidney; season with salt and pepper (some add a little flour to thicken the gravy, but it is not necessary), and then add another layer of steak, kidney, and seasoning. Proceed in this manner till the dish is full, when pour in sufficient water to come within 2 inches of the top of the basin. Moisten the edges of the crust, cover the pudding over, press the two crusts together, that the gravy may not escape, and turn up the overhanging paste. Wring out a cloth in hot water, flour it,

SUSSEX PUDDING-DISH.

and tie up the pudding; put it into boiling water, and let it boil for at least 4 hours. If the water diminishes, always replenish with some, hot in a jug, as the pudding should be kept covered all the time, and not allowed to stop boiling. When the cloth is removed, cut out a round piece in the top of the crust, to prevent the pudding bursting, and send it to table in the basin, either in an ornamental dish, or with a napkin pinned round it. Serve quickly.

Time.—For a pudding with 2 lbs. of steak and 2 kidneys allow 4 hours.

Average cost, 2s. 8d.

Sufficient for 6 persons.

Seasonable all the year, but more suitable in winter.

Note.—Beef-steak pudding may be very much enriched by adding a few oysters or mushrooms. The above recipe was contributed to this work by a Sussex lady, in which county the inhabitants are noted for their savoury puddings. It differs from the general way of making them, as the meat is cut up into very small pieces and the basin is differently shaped: on trial, this pudding will be found far nicer, and more full of gravy, than when laid in large pieces in the dish.

LAMB'S SWEETBREADS, LARDED, AND ASPARAGUS
(an Entree).

757. INGREDIENTS.—2 or 3 sweetbreads, $\frac{1}{2}$ pint of veal stock, white pepper and salt to taste, a small bunch of green onions, 1 blade of pounded mace, thickening of butter and flour, 2 eggs, nearly $\frac{1}{2}$ pint of cream, 1 teaspoonful of minced parsley, a very little grated nutmeg.

Mode.—Soak the sweetbreads in lukewarm water, and put them into a saucepan with sufficient boiling water to cover them, and let them simmer for 10 minutes; then take them out and put them into cold water. Now lard them, lay them in a stewpan, add the stock, seasoning, onions, mace, and a thickening of butter and flour, and stew gently for $\frac{1}{4}$ hour or 20 minutes. Beat up the egg with the cream, to which add the minced parsley and a very little grated nutmeg. Put this to the other ingredients; stir it well till quite hot, but do not let it boil after the cream is added, or it will curdle. Have ready some asparagus-tops, boiled; add these to the sweetbreads, and serve.

Time.—Altogether $\frac{1}{2}$ hour. *Average cost,* 2s. 6d. to 3s. 6d. each.
Sufficient—3 sweetbreads for 1 entrée.
Seasonable from Easter to Michaelmas.

ANOTHER WAY TO DRESS SWEETBREADS (an Entree).

758. INGREDIENTS.—Sweetbreads, egg and bread crumbs, $\frac{1}{2}$ pint of gravy, No. 442, $\frac{1}{4}$ glass of sherry.

Mode.—Soak the sweetbreads in water for an hour, and throw them into boiling water to render them firm. Let them stew gently for about $\frac{1}{4}$ hour, take them out and put them into a cloth to drain all the water from them. Brush them over with egg, sprinkle them with bread crumbs, and either brown them in the oven or before the fire. Have ready the above quantity of gravy, to which add $\frac{1}{4}$ glass of sherry; dish the sweetbreads, pour the gravy under them, and garnish with water-cresses.

Time.—Rather more than $\frac{1}{2}$ hour. *Average cost,* 2s. 6d. to 3s. 6d. each.
Sufficient—3 sweetbreads for 1 entrée.
Seasonable from Easter to Michaelmas.

VEAL AND HAM PIE.

898. INGREDIENTS.—2 lbs. of veal cutlets, $\frac{1}{4}$ lb. of boiled ham, 2 tablespoonfuls of minced savoury herbs, $\frac{1}{4}$ teaspoonful of grated nutmeg, 2 blades of pounded mace, pepper and salt to taste, a strip of lemon-peel finely minced, the yolks of 2 hard-boiled eggs, $\frac{1}{4}$ pint of water, nearly $\frac{1}{2}$ pint of good strong gravy, puff-crust.

Mode.—Cut the veal into nice square pieces, and put a layer of them at the bottom of a pie-dish; sprinkle over these a portion of the herbs, spices, seasoning, lemon-peel, and the yolks of the eggs cut in slices; put the ham very thin, and put a layer of this in. Proceed in this manner until the dish is full, so arranging it that the ham comes at the top. Lay a puff-paste on the edge of the dish, and pour in about $\frac{1}{4}$ pint of water; cover with crust, ornament it with leaves, brush it over with the yolk of an egg, and bake in a well-heated oven for 1 to 1$\frac{1}{2}$ hour, or longer, should the pie be very large. When it is taken out of the oven, pour in at the top, through a funnel, nearly $\frac{1}{2}$ pint of strong gravy: this should be made sufficiently good that, when cold, it may cut in a firm jelly. This pie may be very much enriched by adding a few mushrooms, oysters, or sweetbreads; but it will be found very good without any of the last-named additions.

Time.—1$\frac{1}{2}$ hour, or longer, should the pie be very large.
Average cost, 3s.
Sufficient for 5 or 6 persons.
Seasonable from March to October.

POULET A LA MARENGO.

949. INGREDIENTS.—1 large fowl, 4 tablespoonfuls of salad oil, 1 tablespoonful of flour, 1 pint of stock No. 105, or water, about 20 mushroom-buttons, salt and pepper to taste, 1 teaspoonful of powdered sugar, a very small piece of garlic.

Mode.—Cut the fowl into 8 or 10 pieces; put them with the oil into a stewpan, and brown them over a moderate fire; dredge in the above proportion of flour; when that is browned, pour in the stock or water; let it simmer very slowly for rather more than $\frac{1}{2}$ hour, and skim off the fat as it rises to the top; add the mushrooms; season with salt, pepper, garlic, and sugar; take out the fowl, which arrange pyramidically on the dish, with the inferior joints at the bottom. Reduce the sauce by boiling it quickly over the fire, keeping it stirred until sufficiently thick to adhere to the back of a spoon; pour over the fowl, and serve.

Time.—Altogether 50 minutes. *Average cost,* 3s. 6d.
Sufficient for 3 or 4 persons.
Seasonable at any time.

A FOWL À LA MARENGO.—The following is the origin of the well-known dish Poulet à la Marengo:—On the evening of the battle the first consul was very hungry after the agitation of the day, and a fowl was ordered with all expedition. The fowl was procured, but there was no butter at hand, and unluckily none could be found in the neighbourhood. There was oil in abundance, however; and the cook having poured a certain quantity into his skillet, put in the fowl, with a clove of garlic and other seasoning, with a little white wine, the best the country afforded; he then garnished it with mushrooms, and served it up hot. This dish proved the second conquest of the day, as the first consul found it most agreeable to his palate, and expressed his satisfaction. Ever since, a fowl à la Marengo is a favourite dish with all lovers of good cheer.

PIGEON PIE (Epsom Grand-Stand Recipe).

975. INGREDIENTS.—1$\frac{1}{2}$ lb. of rump-steak, 2 or 3 pigeons, 3 slices of ham, pepper and salt to taste, 2 oz. of butter, 4 eggs, puff crust.

Mode.—Cut the steak into pieces about 3 inches square, and with it line the bottom of a pie-dish, seasoning it well with pepper and salt. Clean the pigeons, rub them with pepper and salt inside and out, and put into the body of each rather more than $\frac{1}{2}$ oz. of butter; lay them on the steak, and a piece of ham on each pigeon. Add the yolks of 4 eggs, and half fill the dish with stock; place a border of puff paste round the edge of the dish, put on the cover, and ornament it in any way that may be preferred. Clean three of the feet, and place them in a hole made in the crust at the top: this shows what kind of pie it is. Glaze the crust,—that is to say, brush it over with the yolk of an egg,—and bake it in a well-heated oven for about 1$\frac{1}{4}$ hour. When liked, a seasoning of pounded mace may be added.

Time.—1$\frac{1}{4}$ hour, or rather less. *Average cost,* 5s. 3d.
Sufficient for 5 or 6 persons. *Seasonable* at any time.

PHEASANT CUTLETS.

1040. INGREDIENTS.—2 or 3 pheasants, egg and bread crumbs, cayenne and salt to taste, brown gravy.

Mode.—Procure 3 young pheasants that have been hung a few days; pluck, draw, and wipe them inside; cut them into joints; remove the bones from the best of these; and the backbones, trimmings, &c., put into a stewpan, with a little stock, herbs, vegetables, seasoning, &c., to make the gravy. Flatten and trim the cutlets of a good shape, egg and bread crumb them, broil them over a clear fire, pile them high in the dish, and pour under them the gravy made from the bones, which should be strained, flavoured, and thickened. One of the small bones should be stuck on the point of each cutlet.

Time.—10 minutes. *Average cost,* 2s. 6d. to 3s. each.
Sufficient for 2 entrées.
Seasonable from the 1st of October to the beginning of February.

GROUSE PIE.

1024. INGREDIENTS.—Grouse; cayenne, salt, and pepper to taste; 1 lb. of rump-steak, ½ pint of well-seasoned broth, puff paste.

Mode.—Line the bottom of a pie-dish with the rump-steak cut into neat pieces, and, should the grouse be large, cut them into joints; but, if small, they may be laid in the pie whole; season highly with salt, cayenne, and black pepper; pour in the broth, and cover with a puff paste; brush the crust over with the yolk of an egg, and bake from ¾ to 1 hour. If the grouse is cut into joints, the backbones and trimmings will make the gravy, by stewing them with an onion, a little sherry, a bunch of herbs, and a blade of mace: this should be poured in after the pie is baked.

Time.—¾ to 1 hour.

Average cost, exclusive of the grouse, which are seldom bought, 1s. 9d.

Seasonable from the 12th of August to the beginning of December.

TO MAKE SAUSAGES.
(Author's Oxford Recipe.)

837. INGREDIENTS.—1 lb. of pork, fat and lean, without skin or gristle; 1 lb. of lean veal, 1 lb. of beef suet, ½ lb. of bread crumbs, the rind of ½ lemon, 1 small nutmeg, 6 sage-leaves, 1 teaspoonful of pepper, 2 teaspoonfuls of salt, ½ teaspoonful of savory, ½ teaspoonful of marjoram.

Mode.—Chop the pork, veal, and suet finely together, add the bread crumbs, lemon-peel (which should be well minced), and a small nutmeg grated. Wash and chop the sage-leaves very finely; add these with the remaining ingredients to the sausage-meat, and when thoroughly mixed, either put the meat into skins, or, when wanted for table, form it into little cakes, which should be floured and fried.

Average cost, for this quantity, 2s. 6d.

Sufficient for about 30 moderate-sized sausages.

Seasonable from October to March.

FORCEMEAT FOR VEAL, TURKEYS, FOWLS, HARE, &c.

417. INGREDIENTS.—2 oz. of ham or lean bacon, ¼ lb. of suet, the rind of half a lemon, 1 teaspoonful of minced parsley, 1 teaspoonful of minced sweet herbs; salt, cayenne, and pounded mace to taste; 6 oz. of bread crumbs, 2 eggs.

Mode.—Shred the ham or bacon, chop the suet, lemon-peel, and herbs, taking particular care that all be very finely minced; add a seasoning to taste, of salt, cayenne, and mace, and blend all thoroughly together with the bread crumbs, before wetting. Now beat and strain the eggs, work these up with the other ingredients, and the forcemeat will be ready for use. When it is made into balls, fry of a nice brown, in boiling lard, or put them on a tin and bake for ¼ hour in a moderate oven. As we have stated before, no one flavour should predominate greatly, and the forcemeat should be of sufficient body to cut with a knife, and yet not dry and heavy. For very delicate forcemeat, it is advisable to pound the ingredients together before binding with the egg; but for ordinary cooking, mincing very finely answers the purpose.

Average cost, 8d.

Sufficient for a turkey, a moderate-sized fillet of veal, or a hare.

BASIL.

Note.—In forcemeat for HARE, the liver of the animal is sometimes added. Boil for 5 minutes, mince it very small, and mix it with the other ingredients. If it should be in an unsound state, it must be on no account made use of.

SWEET HERBS.—Those most usually employed for purposes of cooking, such as the flavouring of soups, sauces, forcemeats, &c are thyme, sage, mint, marjoram, savory, and basil. Other sweet herbs are cultivated for purposes of medicine and perfumery: they are most grateful both to the organs of taste and smelling; and to the aroma derived from them is due, in a great measure, the sweet and exhilarating fragrance of our "flowery meads." In town, sweet herbs have to be procured at the greengrocers' or herbalists', whilst, in the country, the garden should furnish all that are wanted, the cook taking great care to have some dried in the autumn for her use throughout the winter months.

TOAD-IN-THE-HOLE (Cold Meat Cookery).

743. INGREDIENTS.—6 oz. of flour, 1 pint of milk, 3 eggs, butter, a few slices of cold mutton, pepper and salt to taste, 2 kidneys.

Mode.—Make a smooth batter of flour, milk, and eggs in the above proportion; butter a baking-dish, and pour in the batter. Into this place a few slices of cold mutton, previously well seasoned, and the kidneys, which should be cut into rather small pieces; bake about 1 hour, or rather longer, and send it to table in the dish it was baked in. Oysters or mushrooms may be substituted for the kidneys, and will be found exceedingly good.

Time.—Rather more than 1 hour.

Average cost, exclusive of the cold meat, 8d.

Seasonable at any time.

VEGETABLES

BAKED TOMATOES.
(Excellent.)

1158. INGREDIENTS.—8 or 10 tomatoes, pepper and salt to taste, 2 oz. of butter, bread crumbs.

Mode.—Take off the stalks from the tomatoes; cut them into thick slices, and put them into a deep baking-dish; add a plentiful seasoning of pepper and salt, and butter in the above proportion; cover the whole with bread crumbs; drop over these a little clarified butter; bake in a moderate oven from 20 minutes to ½ hour, and serve very hot. This vegetable, dressed as above, is an exceedingly nice accompaniment to all kinds of roast meat. The tomatoes, instead of being cut in slices, may be baked whole; but they will take rather longer time to cook.

Time.—20 minutes to ¼ hour.

Average cost, in full season, 9d. per basket.

Sufficient for 5 or 6 persons.

SPINACH DRESSED WITH CREAM, a la Francaise.

1156. INGREDIENTS.—2 pailfuls of spinach, 2 tablespoonfuls of salt, 2 oz. of butter, 8 tablespoonfuls of cream, 1 small teaspoonful of pounded sugar, a very little grated nutmeg.

Mode.—Boil and drain the spinach as in recipe No. 1155; chop it finely, and put it into a stewpan with the butter; stir over a gentle fire, and, when the butter has dried away, add the remaining ingredients, and simmer for about 5 minutes. Previously to adding the cream, boil it first, in case it should curdle. Serve on a hot dish, and garnish either with sippets of toasted bread or leaves of puff-paste.

SPINACH.

Time.—10 to 15 minutes to boil the spinach; 10 minutes to stew with the cream.

Average cost for the above quantity, 8*d.*

Sufficient for 5 or 6 persons.

Seasonable. — Spring spinach from March to July; winter spinach from November to March.

SPINACH.—This is a Persian plant. It has been cultivated in our gardens about two hundred years, and is the most wholesome of vegetables. It is not very nutritious, but is very easily digested. It is very light and laxative. Wonderful properties have been ascribed to spinach. It is an excellent vegetable, and very beneficial to health. Plainly dressed, it is a resource for the poor; prepared luxuriantly, it is a choice dish for the rich.

CUCUMBERS A LA POULETTE.

1112. INGREDIENTS.—2 or 3 cucumbers, salt and vinegar, 2 oz. of butter, flour, $\frac{1}{2}$ pint of broth, 1 teaspoonful of minced parsley, a lump of sugar, the yolks of 2 eggs, salt and pepper to taste.

Mode.—Pare and cut the cucumbers into slices of an equal thickness, and let them remain in a pickle of salt and vinegar for $\frac{1}{2}$ hour; then drain them in a cloth, and put them into a stewpan with the butter. Fry them over a brisk fire, but do not brown them, and then dredge over them a little flour; add the broth, skim off all the fat, which will rise to the surface, and boil gently until the gravy is somewhat reduced; but the cucumber should not be broken. Stir in the yolks of the eggs, add the parsley, sugar, and a seasoning of pepper and salt; bring the whole to the *point of boiling*, and serve.

Time.—Altogether, 1 hour.

Average cost, when cheapest, 4*d.* each.

Sufficient for 5 or 6 persons.

Seasonable in July, August, and September; but may be had, forced, from the beginning of March.

POTATOES A LA MAITRE D'HOTEL.

1144. INGREDIENTS.—Potatoes, salt and water; to every 6 potatoes allow 1 tablespoonful of minced parsley, 2 oz. of butter, pepper and salt to taste, 4 tablespoonfuls of gravy, 2 tablespoonfuls of lemon-juice.

Mode.—Wash the potatoes clean, and boil them in salt and water by recipe No. 1138; when they are done, drain them, let them cool; then peel and cut the potatoes into thick slices: if these are too thin, they would break in the sauce. Put the butter into a stewpan with the pepper, salt, gravy, and parsley; mix these ingredients well together, put in the potatoes, shake them two or three times, that they may be well covered with the sauce, and, when quite hot through, squeeze in the lemon-juice, and serve.

Time.—$\frac{1}{2}$ to $\frac{3}{4}$ hour to boil the potatoes; 10 minutes for them to heat in the sauce.

Average cost, 4*s.* per bushel.

Sufficient for 3 persons. *Seasonable* all the year.

POTATO SNOW.

1148. INGREDIENTS.—Potatoes, salt, and water.

Mode.—Choose large white potatoes, as free from spots as possible; boil them in their skins in salt and water until perfectly tender; drain and *dry them thoroughly* by the side of the fire, and peel them. Put a hot dish before the fire, rub the potatoes through a coarse sieve on to this dish; do not touch them afterwards, or the flakes will fall, and serve as hot as possible.

Time.—$\frac{1}{2}$ to $\frac{3}{4}$ hour to boil the potatoes.

Average cost, 4*s.* per bushel.

Sufficient,—6 potatoes for 3 persons.

Seasonable at any time.

THE POTATO AS AN ARTICLE OF HUMAN FOOD.—This valuable esculent, next to wheat, is of the greatest importance in the eye of the political economist. From no other crop that can be cultivated does the public derive so much benefit; and it has been demonstrated that an acre of potatoes will feed double the number of people that can be fed from an acre of wheat.

PUDDINGS

SUET CRUST, for Pies or Puddings.

1215. INGREDIENTS.—To every lb. of flour allow 5 or 6 oz. of beef suet, $\frac{1}{2}$ pint of water.

Mode.—Free the suet from skin and shreds; chop it extremely fine, and rub it well into the flour; work the whole to a smooth paste with the above proportion of water; roll it out, and it is ready for use. This crust is quite rich enough for ordinary purposes, but when a better one is desired, use from $\frac{1}{2}$ to $\frac{3}{4}$ lb. of suet to every lb. of flour. Some cooks, for rich crusts, pound the suet in a mortar, with a small quantity of butter. It should then be laid on the paste in small pieces, the same as for puff-crust, and will be found exceedingly nice for hot tarts. 5 oz. of suet to every lb. of flour will make a very good crust; and even $\frac{1}{4}$ lb. will answer very well for children, or where the crust is wanted very plain.

Average cost, 5*d.* per lb.

BAKED APPLE DUMPLINGS (a Plain Family Dish).

1225. INGREDIENTS.—6 apples, $\frac{3}{4}$ lb. of suet-crust No. 1215, sugar to taste.

Mode.—Pare and take out the cores of the apples without dividing them, and make $\frac{1}{2}$ lb. of suet-crust by recipe No. 1215; roll the apples in the crust, previously sweetening them with moist sugar, and taking care to join the paste nicely. When they are formed into round balls, put them on a tin, and bake them for about $\frac{1}{2}$ hour, or longer should the apples be very large; arrange them pyramidically on a dish, and sift over them some pounded white sugar. These may be made richer by using one of the puff-pastes instead of suet.

Time.—From $\frac{1}{2}$ to $\frac{3}{4}$ hour, or longer. *Average cost,* $1\frac{1}{2}$*d.* each.

Sufficient for 4 persons.

Seasonable from August to March, but flavourless after the end of January

AUNT NELLY'S PUDDING.

1224. INGREDIENTS.—½ lb. of flour, ½ lb. of treacle, ½ lb. of suet, the rind and juice of 1 lemon, a few strips of candied lemon-peel, 3 tablespoonfuls of cream, 2 eggs.

Mode.—Chop the suet finely; mix with it the flour, treacle, lemon-peel minced, and candied lemon-peel; add the cream, lemon-juice, and 2 well-beaten eggs; beat the pudding well, put it into a buttered basin, tie it down with a cloth, and boil from 3½ to 4 hours.

Time.—3½ to 4 hours. *Average cost,* 1*s.* 2*d.*

Sufficient for 5 or 6 persons.

Seasonable at any time, but more suitable for a winter pudding.

TREACLE, OR MOLASSES.—Treacle is the uncrystallizable part of the saccharine juice drained from the Muscovado sugar, and is either naturally so or rendered uncrystallizable through some defect in the process of boiling. As it contains a large quantity of sweet or saccharine principle and is cheap, it is of great use as an article of domestic economy. Children are especially fond of it; and it is accounted wholesome. It is also useful for making beer, rum, and the very dark syrups.

BARONESS PUDDING.

(*Author's Recipe.*)

1244. INGREDIENTS.—¾ lb. of suet, ¾ lb. of raisins weighed after being stoned, ¾ lb. of flour, ½ pint of milk, ¼ saltspoonful of salt.

Mode.—Prepare the suet, by carefully freeing it from skin, and chop it finely; stone the raisins, and cut them in halves, and mix both these ingredients with the salt and flour; moisten the whole with the above proportion of milk, stir the mixture well, and tie the pudding in a floured cloth, which has been previously wrung out in boiling water. Put the pudding into a saucepan of boiling water, and let it boil, without ceasing, 4½ hours. Serve merely with plain sifted sugar, a little of which may be sprinkled over the pudding.

Time.—4½ hours. *Average cost,* 1*s.* 4*d.*

Sufficient for 7 or 8 persons.

Seasonable in winter, when fresh fruit is not obtainable.

Note.—This pudding the editress cannot too highly recommend. The recipe was kindly given to her family by a lady who bore the title here prefixed to it; and with all who have partaken of it, it is an especial favourite. Nothing is of greater consequence, in the above directions, than attention to the time of boiling, which should never be *less* than that mentioned.

COLLEGE PUDDINGS.

1263. INGREDIENTS.—1 pint of bread crumbs, 6 oz. of finely-chopped suet, ¼ lb. of currants, a few thin slices of candied peel, 3 oz. of sugar, ¼ nutmeg, 3 eggs, 4 tablespoonfuls of brandy.

Mode.—Put the bread crumbs into a basin; add the suet, currants, candied peel, sugar, and nutmeg, grated, and stir these ingredients until they are thoroughly mixed. Beat up the eggs, moisten the pudding with these, and put in the brandy; beat well for a few minutes, then form the mixture into round balls or egg-shaped pieces; fry these in hot butter or lard, letting them stew in it until thoroughly done, and turn them two or three times, till of a fine light brown; drain them on a piece of blotting-paper before the fire; dish, and serve with wine sauce.

Time.—15 to 20 minutes. *Average cost,* 1*s.*

Sufficient for 7 or 8 puddings. *Seasonable* at any time.

AN EXCELLENT WINE SAUCE FOR PUDDINGS.

1362. INGREDIENTS.—The yolks of 4 eggs, 1 teaspoonful of flour, 2 oz. of pounded sugar, 2 oz. of fresh butter, ¼ saltspoonful of salt, ½ pint of sherry or Madeira.

Mode.—Put the butter and flour into a saucepan, and stir them over the fire until the former thickens; then add the sugar, salt, and wine, and mix these ingredients well together. Separate the yolks from the whites of 4 eggs; beat up the former, and stir them briskly to the sauce; let it remain over the fire until it is on the point of simmering; but do not allow it to boil, or it will instantly curdle. This sauce is delicious with plum, marrow, or bread puddings; but should be served separately, and not poured over the pudding.

Time.—From 5 to 7 minutes to thicken the butter; about 5 minutes to stir the sauce over the fire.

Average cost, 1*s.* 10*d.* *Sufficient* for 7 or 8 persons.

LEMON MINCEMEAT.

1293. INGREDIENTS.—2 large lemons, 6 large apples, ½ lb. of suet, 1 lb. of currants, ½ lb. of sugar, 2 oz. of candied lemon-peel, 1 oz. of citron, mixed spice to taste.

Mode.—Pare the lemons, squeeze them, and boil the peel until tender enough to mash. Add to the mashed lemon-peel the apples, which should be pared, cored, and minced; the chopped suet, currants, sugar, sliced peel, and spice. Strain the lemon-juice to these ingredients, stir the mixture well, and put it in a jar with a closely-fitting lid. Stir occasionally, and in a week or 10 days the mincemeat will be ready for use.

Average cost, 2*s.*

Sufficient for 18 large or 24 small pies.

Seasonable.—Make this about the beginning of December.

CHRISTMAS PLUM-PUDDING.

(*Very Good.*)

1328. INGREDIENTS.—1½ lb. of raisins, ½ lb. of currants, ½ lb. of mixed peel, ¾ lb. of bread crumbs, ¾ lb. of suet, 8 eggs, 1 wineglassful of brandy.

Mode.—Stone and cut the raisins in halves, but do not chop them; wash, pick, and dry the currants, and mince the suet finely; cut the candied peel into thin slices, and grate down the bread into fine crumbs. When all these dry ingredients are prepared, mix them well together; then moisten the mixture with the eggs, which should be well beaten, and the brandy; stir well, that everything may be very thoroughly blended, and *press* the pudding into a buttered mould; tie it down tightly with a floured cloth, and boil for 5 or 6 hours. It may be boiled in a cloth without a mould, and will require the same time allowed for cooking. As Christmas puddings are usually made a few days before they are required for table, when the pudding is taken out of the pot, hang it up immediately, and put a plate or saucer underneath to catch the water that may drain from it. The day it is to be eaten, plunge it into boiling water, and keep it boiling for at least 2 hours; then turn it out of the mould, and serve with brandy-sauce. On Christmas-day a sprig of holly is usually placed in the middle of the pudding, and about a wineglassful of brandy poured round it, which, at the moment of serving, is lighted, and the pudding thus brought to table encircled in flame.

CHRISTMAS PLUM-PUDDING IN MOULD

Time.—5 or 6 hours the first time of boiling; 2 hours the day it is to be served.

Average cost, 4s.

Sufficient for a quart mould for 7 or 8 persons.

Seasonable on the 25th of December, and on various festive occasions till March.

Note.—Five or six of these puddings should be made at one time, as they

TO FROST HOLLY-LEAVES, for garnishing and decorating Dessert and Supper Dishes.

1545.—INGREDIENTS.—Sprigs of holly, oiled butter, coarsely-powdered sugar.

Mode.—Procure some nice sprigs of holly; pick the leaves from the stalks, and wipe them with a clean cloth free from all moisture; then place them on a dish near the fire, to get thoroughly dry, but not too near to shrivel the leaves; dip them into oiled butter, sprinkle over them some coarsely-powdered sugar, and dry them before the fire. They should be kept in a dry place, as the least damp would spoil their appearance.

Time.—About 10 minutes to dry before the fire.

Seasonable.—These may be made at any time; but are more suitable for winter garnishes, when fresh flowers are not easily obtained.

VERY GOOD PUFF-PASTE.

1205. INGREDIENTS.—To every lb. of flour allow 1 lb. of butter, and not quite ½ pint of water.

Mode.—Carefully weigh the flour and butter, and have the exact proportion; squeeze the butter well, to extract the water from it, and afterwards wring it in a clean cloth, that no moisture may remain. Sift the flour; see that it is perfectly dry, and proceed in the following manner to make the paste, using a very *clean* pasteboard and rolling-pin:—Supposing the quantity to be 1 lb. of flour, work the whole into a smooth paste, with not quite ½ pint of water, using a knife to mix it with: the proportion of this latter ingredient must be regulated by the discretion of the cook; if too much be added, the paste, when baked, will be tough. Roll it out until it is of an equal thickness of about an inch; break 4 oz. of the butter into small pieces; place these on the paste, sift over it a little flour, fold it over, roll out again, and put another 4 oz. of butter. Repeat the rolling and buttering until the paste has been rolled out 4 times, or equal quantities of flour and butter have been used. Do not omit, every time the paste is rolled out, to dredge a little flour over that and the rolling-pin, to prevent both from sticking. Handle the paste as lightly as possible, and do not press heavily upon it with the rolling-pin. The next thing to be considered is the oven, as the baking of pastry requires particular attention. Do not put it into the oven until it is sufficiently hot to raise the paste; for the best-prepared paste, if not properly baked, will be good for nothing. Brushing the paste as often as rolled out, and the pieces of butter placed thereon, with the white of an egg, assists it to rise in *leaves* or *flakes*. As this is the great beauty of puff-paste, it is as well to try this method.

Average cost, 1s. 4d. per lb.

BUTTER.—About the second century of the Christian era, butter was placed by Galen amongst the useful medical agents; and about a century before him, Dioscorides mentioned that he had noticed that fresh butter, made of ewes' and goats' milk, was served at meals instead of oil, and that it took the place of fat in making pastry. Thus we have undoubted authority that, eighteen hundred years ago, there existed a knowledge of the

COMMON CRUST FOR RAISED PIES.

1217. INGREDIENTS.—To every lb. of flour allow ½ pint of water, 1¼ oz. of butter, 1⅓ oz. of lard, ½ saltspoonful of salt.

Mode.—Put into a saucepan the water; when it boils, add the butter and lard; and when these are melted, make a hole in the middle of the flour; pour in the water gradually; beat it well with a wooden spoon, and be particular in not making the paste too soft. When it is well mixed, knead it with the hands until quite stiff, dredging a little flour over the paste and board, to prevent them from sticking. When it is well kneaded, place it before the fire, with a cloth covered over it, for a few minutes; it will then be more easily worked into shape. This paste does not taste so nicely as the preceding one, but is worked with greater facility, and answers just as well for raised pies, for the crust is seldom eaten.

Average cost, 5d. per lb.

CREAM, JELLIES & SWEET DISHES

TO MAKE GOOSEBERRY FOOL.

1433. INGREDIENTS.—Green gooseberries; to every pint of pulp add 1 pint of milk, or ½ pint of cream and ½ pint of milk; sugar to taste.

Mode.—Cut the tops and tails off the gooseberries; put them into a jar, with 2 tablespoonfuls of water and a little good moist sugar; set this jar in a saucepan of boiling water, and let it boil until the fruit is soft enough to mash. When done enough, beat it to a pulp, work this pulp through a colander, and stir to every pint the above proportion of milk, or equal quantities of milk and cream. Ascertain if the mixture is sweet enough, and put in plenty of sugar, or it will not be eatable; and in mixing the milk and gooseberries, add the former very gradually to these: serve in a glass dish, or in small glasses. This, although a very old-fashioned and homely dish, is, when well made, very delicious, and, if properly sweetened, a very suitable preparation for children.

Time.—From ¾ to 1 hour. *Average cost*, 6d. per pint, with milk.

Sufficient.—A pint of milk and a pint of gooseberry pulp for 5 or 6 children.

Seasonable in May and June.

A PRETTY DISH OF ORANGES.

1466. INGREDIENTS.—6 large oranges, ¼ lb. of loaf sugar, ¼ pint of water, ¼ pint of cream, 2 tablespoonfuls of any kind of liqueur, sugar to taste.

Mode.—Put the sugar and water into a saucepan, and boil them until the sugar becomes brittle, which may be ascertained by taking up a small quantity in a spoon, and dipping it in cold water; if the sugar is sufficiently boiled, it will easily snap. Peel the oranges, remove as much of the white pith as possible, and divide them into nice-sized slices, without breaking the thin white skin which surrounds the juicy pulp. Place the pieces of orange on small skewers, dip them into the hot sugar, and arrange them in layers round a plain mould, which should be well oiled with the purest salad-oil. The sides of the mould only should be lined with the oranges, and the centre left open for the cream. Let the sugar become firm by cooling; turn the oranges carefully out on a dish, and fill the centre with whipped cream, flavoured with any kind of liqueur, and sweetened with pounded sugar. This is an exceedingly ornamental and nice dish for the supper-table.

Time.—10 minutes to boil the sugar. *Average cost*, 1s. 8d.

Sufficient for 1 mould. *Seasonable* from November to May.

LIQUEUR JELLY.

1449. INGREDIENTS.—1 lb. of lump sugar, 2 oz. of isinglass, 1½ pint of water, the juice of 2 lemons, ⅓ pint of liqueur.

Mode.—Put the sugar, with 1 pint of the water, into a stewpan, and boil them gently by the side of the fire until there is no scum remaining, which must be carefully removed as fast as it rises. Boil the isinglass with the other ½ pint of water, and skim it carefully in the same manner. Strain the lemon-juice, and add it, with the clarified isinglass, to the syrup; put in the liqueur, and bring the whole to the boiling-point. Let the saucepan remain covered by the side of the

OVAL JELLY-MOULD.

fire for a few minutes; then pour the jelly through a bag, put it into a mould, and set the mould in ice until required for table. Dip the mould in hot water, wipe the outside, loosen the jelly by passing a knife round the edges, and turn it out carefully on a dish. Noyeau, Maraschino, Curaçoa, brandy, or any kind of liqueur, answers for this jelly; and, when made with isinglass, liqueur jellies are usually prepared as directed above.

Time.—10 minutes to boil the sugar and water.

Average cost, with the best isinglass, 3s. 6d.

Sufficient to fill a quart mould. *Seasonable* at any time.

BOILED CUSTARDS.

1423. INGREDIENTS.—1 pint of milk, 5 eggs, 3 oz. of loaf sugar, 3 laurel-leaves, or the rind of ½ lemon, or a few drops of essence of vanilla, 1 tablespoonful of brandy.

Mode.—Put the milk into a *lined* saucepan, with the sugar, and whichever of the above flavourings may be preferred (the lemon-rind

CUSTARDS IN GLASSES.

flavours custards most deliciously), and let the milk steep by the side of the fire until it is well flavoured. Bring it to the point of boiling, then strain it into a basin; whisk the eggs well, and, when the milk has cooled a little, stir in the eggs, and *strain* this mixture into a jug. Place this jug in a saucepan of boiling water over the fire; keep stirring the custard *one way* until it thickens; but on no account allow it to reach the boiling-point, as it will instantly curdle and be full of lumps. Take it off the fire, stir in the brandy, and, when this is well mixed with the custard, pour it into glasses, which should be rather more than three-parts full; grate a little nutmeg over the

top, and the dish is ready for table. To make custards look and eat better, ducks' eggs should be used, when obtainable; they add very much to the flavour and richness, and so many are not required as of the ordinary eggs, 4 ducks' eggs to the pint of milk making a delicious custard. When desired extremely rich and good, cream should be substituted for the milk, and double the quantity of eggs used, to those mentioned, omitting the whites.

Time.—½ hour to infuse the lemon-rind, about 10 minutes to stir the custard. *Average cost*, 8d.

Sufficient to fill 8 custard-glasses. *Seasonable* at any time.

TIPSY CAKE.

1487. INGREDIENTS.—1 moulded sponge- or Savoy-cake, sufficient sweet wine or sherry to soak it, 6 tablespoonfuls of brandy, 2 oz. of sweet almonds, 1 pint of rich custard.

Mode.—Procure a cake that is three or four days old,—either sponge, Savoy, or rice answering for the purpose of a tipsy cake. Cut the bottom of the cake level, to make it stand firm in the dish; make a small hole in the centre, and pour in and over the cake sufficient sweet wine or sherry, mixed with the above proportion of brandy, to soak it nicely. When the cake is well soaked, blanch and cut the almonds into strips, stick them all over the cake, and pour round it a good custard, made by recipe No. 1423, allowing 8 eggs instead of 5 to the pint of milk. The cakes are sometimes crumbled and soaked, and a whipped cream heaped over them, the same as for trifles.

TIPSY CAKE.

Time.—About 2 hours to soak the cake. *Average cost*, 4s. 6d.

Sufficient for 1 dish. *Seasonable* at any time.

TO MAKE A TRIFLE

1489. INGREDIENTS.—For the whip, 1 pint of cream, 3 oz. of pounded sugar, the whites of 2 eggs, a small glass of sherry or raisin wine. For the trifle, 1 pint of custard, made with 8 eggs to a pint of milk; 6 small sponge-cakes, or 6 slices of sponge-cake; 12 macaroons, 2 dozen ratafias, 2 oz. of sweet almonds, the grated rind of 1 lemon, a layer of raspberry or strawberry jam, ½ pint of sherry or sweet wine, 6 tablespoonfuls of brandy.

Mode.—The whip to lay over the top of the trifle should be made the day before it is required for table, as the flavour is better, and it is

TRIFLE.

much more solid than when prepared the same day. Put into a large bowl the pounded sugar, the whites of the eggs, which should be beaten to a stiff froth, a glass of sherry or sweet wine, and the cream. Whisk these ingredients well in a cool place, and take off the froth with a skimmer as fast as it rises, and put it on a sieve to drain; continue the whisking till there is sufficient of the whip, which must be put away in a cool place to drain. The next day, place the sponge-cakes, macaroons, and ratafias at the bottom of a trifle-dish; pour over them ½ pint of sherry or sweet wine, mixed with 6 tablespoonfuls of brandy, and, should this proportion of wine not be found quite sufficient, add a little more, as the cakes should be well soaked. Over the cakes put the grated lemon-rind, the sweet almonds, blanched and cut into strips, and a layer of raspberry or strawberry jam. Make a good custard by recipe No. 1423, using 8 instead of 5 eggs to the pint of milk, and let this cool a little; then pour it over the cakes, &c. The whip being made the day previously, and the trifle prepared, there remains nothing to do now but heap the whip lightly over the top: this should stand as high as possible, and it may be garnished with strips of bright currant jelly, crystallized sweetmeats, or flowers; the small coloured comfits are sometimes used for the purpose of garnishing a trifle, but they are now considered rather old-fashioned. (See coloured plate, V 1.)

Average cost, with cream at 1s. per pint, 5s. 6d.

Sufficient for 1 trifle. *Seasonable* at any time.

WHIPPPED SYLLABUBS.

1493. INGREDIENTS.—½ pint of cream, ¼ pint of sherry, half that quantity of brandy, the juice of ½ lemon, a little grated nutmeg, 3 oz. of pounded sugar, whipped cream the same as for trifle No. 1489.

Mode.—Mix all the ingredients together, put the syllabub into glasses, and over the top of them heap a little whipped cream, made in the same manner as for trifle No. 1489. Solid syllabub is made by whisking or milling the mixture to a stiff froth, and putting it in the glasses, without the whipped cream at the top.

Average cost, 1s. 8d.

Sufficient to fill 8 or 9 glasses. *Seasonable* at any time.

BREAD, BISCUITS

EXCELLENT ROLLS.

1723. INGREDIENTS.—To every lb. of flour allow 1 oz. of butter, ¼ pint of milk, 1 large teaspoonful of yeast, a little salt.

Mode.—Warm the butter in the milk, add to it the yeast and salt, and mix these ingredients well together. Put the flour into a pan, stir in the above ingredients, and let the dough rise, covered in a warm place. Knead it well, make it into rolls, let them rise again for a few minutes, and bake in a quick oven.

ROLLS.

Richer rolls may be made by adding 1 or 2 eggs and a larger proportion of butter, and their appearance improved by brushing the tops over with yolk of egg or a little milk.

Time.—1 lb. of flour, divided into 6 rolls, from 15 to 20 minutes.

DESSERT BISCUITS, which may be flavoured with Ground Ginger, Cinnamon, &c. &c.

1742. INGREDIENTS.—1 lb. of flour, ½ lb. of butter, ½ lb. of sifted sugar, the yolks of 6 eggs, flavouring to taste.

Mode.—Put the butter into a basin; warm it, but do not allow it to oil; then with the hand beat it to a cream. Add the flour by degrees, then the sugar and flavouring, and moisten the whole with the yolks of the eggs, which should previously be well beaten. When all the ingredients are thoroughly incorporated, drop the mixture from a spoon on to a buttered paper, leaving a distance between each cake, as they spread as soon as they begin to get warm. Bake in rather a slow oven from 12 to 18 minutes, and do not let the biscuits acquire too much colour. In making the above quantity, half may be flavoured with ground ginger and the other half with essence of lemon or currants, to make a variety. With whatever the preparation is flavoured, so are the biscuits called; and an endless variety may be made in this manner.

Time.—12 to 18 minutes, or rather longer, in a very slow oven.

Average cost, 1s. 6d.

Sufficient to make from 3 to 4 dozen cakes.

Seasonable at any time.

SCOTCH SHORTBREAD.

1780. INGREDIENTS.—2 lbs. of flour, 1 lb. of butter, ¼ lb. of pounded loaf sugar, ½ oz. of caraway seeds, 1 oz. of sweet almonds, a few strips of candied orange-peel.

Mode.—Beat the butter to a cream, gradually dredge in the flour, and add the sugar, caraway seeds, and sweet almonds, which should

SHORTBREAD.

be blanched and cut into small pieces. Work the paste until it is quite smooth, and divide it into six pieces. Put each cake on a separate piece of paper, roll the paste out square to the thickness of about an inch, and pinch it upon all sides. Prick it well, and ornament with one or two strips of candied orange-peel. Put the cakes into a good oven, and bake them from 25 to 30 minutes.

Time.—25 to 30 minutes. *Average cost*, for this quantity, 2s.

Sufficient to make 6 cakes. *Seasonable* at any time.

Note.—Where the flavour of the caraway seeds is disliked, omit them, and add rather a larger proportion of candied peel.

BEVERAGES

CHAMPAGNE-CUP.

1832. INGREDIENTS.—1 quart bottle of champagne, 2 bottles of soda-water, 1 liqueur-glass of brandy or Curaçoa, 2 tablespoonfuls of powdered sugar, 1 lb. of pounded ice, a sprig of green borage.

Mode.—Put all the ingredients into a silver cup; stir them together, and serve the same as claret-cup No. 1831. Should the above proportion of sugar not be found sufficient to suit some tastes, increase the quantity. When borage is not easily obtainable, substitute for it a few slices of cucumber-rind.

Seasonable.—Suitable for pic-nics, balls, weddings, and other festive occasions

CHAMPAGNE.—This, the most celebrated of French wines, is the produce chiefly of the province of that name, and is generally understood in England to be a brisk, effervescing, or sparkling white wine, of a very fine flavour; but this is only one of the varieties of this class. There is both red and white champagne, and each of these may be either still or brisk. There are the sparkling wines (*mousseux*), and the still wines (*non-mousseux*). The brisk are in general the most highly esteemed, or, at least, are the most popular in this country, on account of their delicate flavour and the agreeable pungency which they derive from the carbonic acid they contain, and to which they owe their briskness.

GINGER BEER.

1833. **INGREDIENTS.**—$2\frac{1}{2}$ lbs. of loaf sugar, $1\frac{1}{2}$ oz. of bruised ginger, 1 oz. of cream of tartar, the rind and juice of 2 lemons, 3 gallons of boiling water, 2 large tablespoonfuls of thick and fresh brewer's yeast.

Mode.—Peel the lemons, squeeze the juice, strain it, and put the peel and juice into a large earthen pan, with the bruised ginger, cream of tartar, and loaf sugar. Pour over these ingredients 3 gallons of *boiling* water; let it stand until just warm, when add the yeast, which should be thick and perfectly fresh. Stir the contents of the pan well, and let them remain near the fire all night, covering the pan over with a cloth. The next day skim off the yeast, and pour the liquor carefully into another vessel, leaving the sediment; then bottle immediately, and tie the corks down, and in 3 days the ginger beer will be fit for use. For some tastes, the above proportion of sugar may be found rather too large, when it may be diminished; but the beer will not keep so long good.

Average cost for this quantity, 2*s.*; or $\frac{1}{2}$*d.* per bottle.

Sufficient to fill 4 dozen ginger-beer bottles.

Seasonable.—This should be made during the summer months.

CLARET-CUP.

1831. **INGREDIENTS.**—1 bottle of claret, 1 bottle of soda-water, about $\frac{1}{2}$ lb. of pounded ice, 4 tablespoonfuls of powdered sugar, $\frac{1}{4}$ teaspoonful of grated nutmeg, 1 liqueur-glass of Maraschino, a sprig of green borage.

CLARET-CUP.

Mode.—Put all the ingredients into a silver cup, regulating the proportion of ice by the state of the weather: if very warm, a larger quantity would be necessary. Hand the cup round with a clean napkin passed through one of the handles, that the edge of the cup may be wiped after each guest has partaken of the contents thereof.

Seasonable in summer.

TO MAKE NEGUS.

1835. **INGREDIENTS.**—To every pint of port wine allow 1 quart of boiling water, $\frac{1}{4}$ lb. of sugar, 1 lemon, grated nutmeg to taste.

Mode.—As this beverage is more usually drunk at children's parties than at any other, the wine need not be very old or expensive for the purpose, a new fruity wine answering very well for it. Put the wine into a jug, rub some lumps of sugar (equal to $\frac{1}{4}$ lb.) on the lemon-rind until all the yellow part of the skin is absorbed, then squeeze the juice, and strain it. Add the sugar and lemon-juice to the port wine, with the grated nutmeg; pour over it the boiling water, cover the jug, and, when the beverage has cooled a little, it will be fit for use. Negus may also be made of sherry, or any other sweet white wine, but is more usually made of port than of any other beverage.

Sufficient.—Allow 1 pint of wine, with the other ingredients in proportion, for a party of 9 or 10 children.

TO MAKE HOT PUNCH.

1839. INGREDIENTS.—$\frac{1}{2}$ pint of rum, $\frac{1}{2}$ pint of brandy, $\frac{1}{4}$ lb. of sugar, 1 large lemon, $\frac{1}{2}$ teaspoonful of nutmeg, 1 pint of boiling water.

Mode.—Rub the sugar over the lemon until it has absorbed all the yellow part of the skin, then put the sugar into a punchbowl; add the lemon-juice (free from pips), and mix these two ingredients well together. Pour over them the boiling water, stir well together, add the rum, brandy, and nutmeg; mix thoroughly, and the punch will be ready to serve. It is very important in making good punch that all the ingredients are thoroughly incorporated; and, to insure success, the processes of mixing must be diligently attended to.

PUNCH-BOWL AND LADLE.

Sufficient.—Allow a quart for 4 persons; but this information must be taken *cum grano salis;* for the capacities of persons for this kind of beverage are generally supposed to vary considerably.

PUNCH is a beverage made of various spirituous liquors or wine, hot water, the acid juice of fruits, and sugar. It is considered to be very intoxicating; but this is probably because the spirit, being partly sheathed by the mucilaginous juice and the sugar, its strength does not appear to the taste so great as it really is. Punch, which was almost universally drunk among the middle classes about fifty or sixty years ago, has almost disappeared from our domestic tables, being superseded by wine. There are many different varieties of punch. It is sometimes kept cold in bottles, and makes a most agreeable summer drink. In Scotland, instead of the Madeira or sherry generally used in its manufacture, whiskey is substituted, and then its insidious properties are more than usually felt. Where fresh lemons cannot be had for punch or similar beverages, crystallized citric acid and a few drops of the essence of lemon will be very nearly the same thing. In the composition of "Regent's punch," champagne, brandy, and *veritable Martinique* are required; "Norfolk punch" requires Seville oranges; "Milk punch" may be extemporized by adding a little hot milk to lemonade, and then straining it through a jelly-bag. Then there are "Wine punch," "Tea punch," and "French punch," made with lemons, spirits, and wine, in fantastic proportions. But of all the compounds of these materials, perhaps, for a *summer* drink, the North-American "mint julep" is the most inviting. Captain Marryat gives the following recipe for its preparation:—"Put into a tumbler about a dozen sprigs of the tender shoots of mint; upon them put a spoonful of white sugar, and equal proportions of peach and common brandy, so as to fill up one third, or, perhaps, a little less; then take rasped or pounded ice, and fill up the tumbler. Epicures rub the lips of the tumbler with a piece of fresh pineapple; and the tumbler itself is very often encrusted outside with stalactites of ice. As the ice melts, you drink." The Virginians, says Captain Marryat, claim the merit of having invented this superb compound; but, from a passage in the "Comus" of Milton, he claims it for his own country.

Epsom
Friday morning

Do not be too late for the
train tomorrow

My dear very dear Sam,
Words cannot
express my delight on
receiving your most
kind and affectionate
epistle, I am only afraid
too kind for me! I little
meant on Wednesday
morning when I parted
from you, I should be
soon have the pleasure
of going out with you
again. Of course I shall

be delighted to accompany
you to the Crystal Palace
I will be on Newerby Bridge
at 1.30 by the same train
I came up before, to
morrow afternoon. Saturday
I will sent from there
They do not seem to
be particularly quick
in postal arrangements
at home, for I did not
receive your note till
this morning. How do you
account for it? I fancy
I could shew to place
for themselves in their

One of the many letters written by
Isabella to her beloved Sam.

Index